LIFE IN

Andrew Donkin

Illustrated by
Clive Goddard

SCHOLASTIC

Find Andrew Donkin at www.andrewdonkin.com

Scholastic Children's Books,
Euston House, 24 Eversholt Street,
London NW1 1DB, UK

A division of Scholastic Ltd
London ~ New York ~ Toronto ~ Sydney ~ Auckland
Mexico City ~ New Delhi ~ Hong Kong

First published as *Dead Famous: Roald Dahl and his Chocolate Factory* in the UK by Scholastic Ltd, 2002
This edition published 2016

ISBN 978 1407 17189 0

Page layout services provided by Quadrum Solutions Ltd, Mumbai, India
Printed and bound by CPI Group (UK) Ltd, Croydon, CR0 4YY

2 4 6 8 10 9 7 5 3

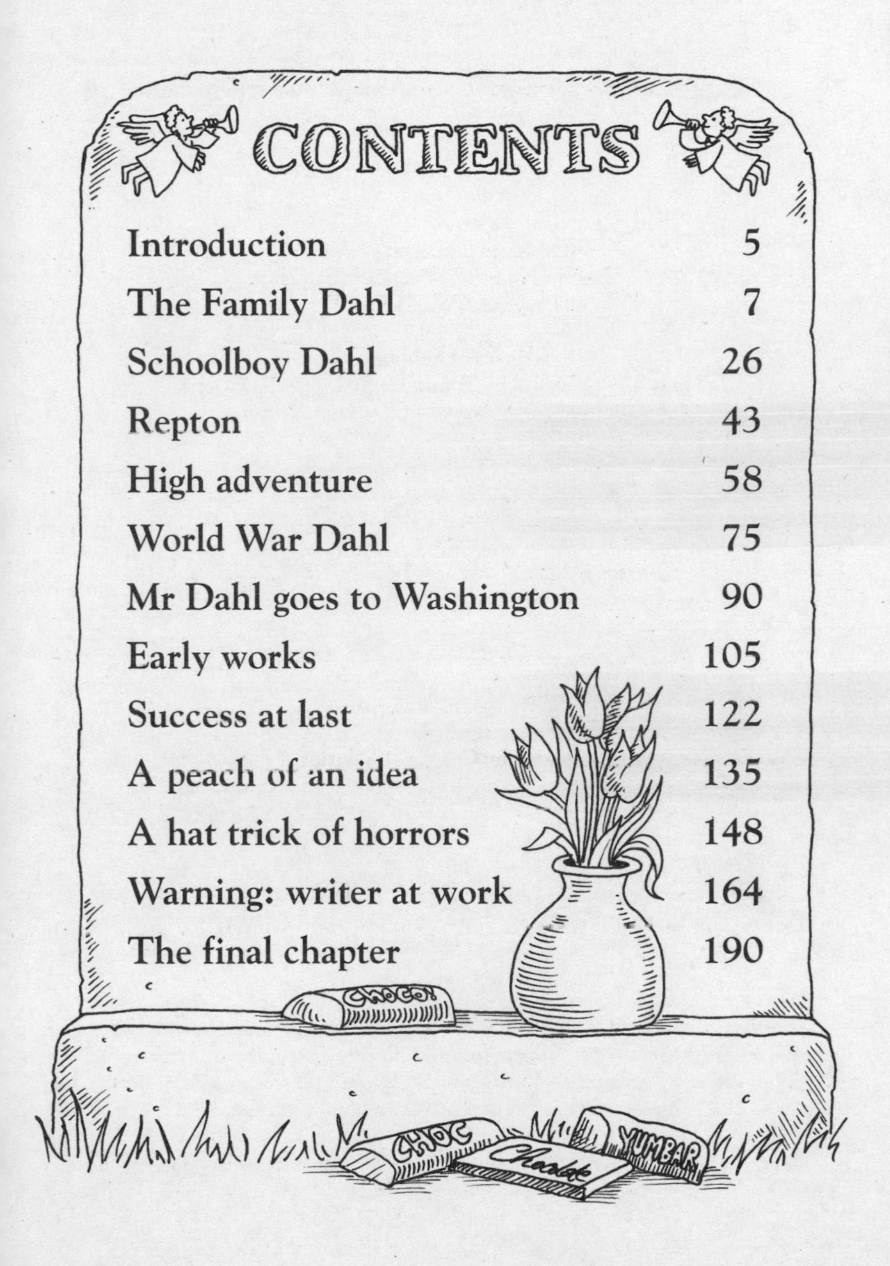

CONTENTS

INTRODUCTION

Roald Dahl is one of greatest children's writers of all time. He's famous for his fantastic stories like *Charlie and the Chocolate Factory*, *James and the Giant Peach*, *The Witches* and *Matilda*, just to mention a few. People love his stories so much that they have also been turned into big budget films and marvellous musical stage shows.

Some people become famous for doing daring deeds during their life. But Roald Dahl was unusual because he became famous by sitting in a small hut in his back garden all day. He spent hour after hour and day after day scribbling words down on a yellow notepad.

But what did he do when he wasn't writing? In this book you'll discover that in the real world, his life was every bit as dangerous, strange, happy, sad and exciting as the stories he wrote.

For example, did you know. . .

- that he was utterly hopeless at English at school?
- that he wrote a James Bond film?
- that doctors had to build him a new nose?

• that he was a champion boxer?

• that he loved practical jokes – the nastier the better?
• that he was a fighter pilot in the Second Word War?
• that he nearly died when he crashed his plane in the desert?
• that he became a spy?

• that one moment he could be kindly and wise, but the next be difficult, dangerous and impossibly rude?

Everybody knows Roald's books have sold millions and billions (and zillions) of copies all over the world, but why do people love his tall tales so much? Where did he get his brilliant ideas about giants and witches and chocolate factories that went into his stories?

This book tells you the true story of the greatest storyteller of them all. You can read Roald's secret diary to find out what he might have said about his life. Then turn to the news-packed pages of the *Dahly Telegraph* to see how a newspaper might have reported things.

Find out about Roald Dahl's life and all the events – big and small – that shaped him AND his stories. . .

THE FAMILY DAHL

Most people probably think Roald Dahl was English. Others might remember him as being from Norway. In fact, Roald was born in Wales, on September 13th 1916, the son of two Norwegians living in Cardiff. But hang on a minute, what on earth were two Norwegians doing living in Wales? For the answer to that we have to go back a bit and find out exactly how Roald's father, Harald Dahl, ended up there. . .

The strange (and marvellous) voyage of Harald Dahl

Roald's father came from a small town in Norway called Sarpsborg. Harald Dahl had just as much ambition as Roald would have when he was grown up, and, together with his younger brother Oscar, Harald decided he wanted to get rich. The brothers knew a small Norwegian town wasn't the place to do it – the town simply wasn't big enough for both of them. In fact, it wasn't big enough for either of them. Against their father's wishes, Harald and Oscar left together to seek their fortunes abroad – in a country that was, well . . . bigger.

The two brothers hotfooted it from their little town and worked their passage on a cargo ship to Calais on the French coast. This was more difficult than it sounds – for a start Harald had suffered a childhood 'mishap' which had meant his left arm had been amputated below the elbow. (Ouch!)

How to lose an arm

Having got to France, the Dahl brothers (with three good arms between them) travelled to Paris for an eyeful of the Eiffel Tower. Roald's future Uncle Oscar didn't stay long – he headed off to a fishing port on the west coast of France and became very rich from a fleet of fishing boats. Harald stayed in Paris and met two very important people. The first was Marie – a young French woman whom he married.

The second was another young man from Norway called Aadnesen. Aadnesen was also very keen on the idea of getting rich, and he and Harald decided to go into business together as shipbrokers. Shipbrokers were people who sold all the things needed to sail a ship – food, materials, tools, and, most importantly, the fuel. (Most important because that's where the money was!) In those days, nearly all ships were powered by steam engines and they ran on coal – tons of it. Harald Dahl and his partner set up their new business in Cardiff, then one of the busiest cargo ports in the whole world. It was a smart move and it wasn't long before their firm was turning a tidy profit.

Harald and his wife Marie set up home together and had a daughter Ellen, and then a son called (no, not Roald, but don't worry, we're getting there) Louis. But sadly, a year after giving birth to Louis, Marie died aged just 29. Harald was devastated. He raised his two children on his own for four years. Then decided he had to do something. He knew his children needed someone to love and look after them (so did he, come to that) and he thought a new wife was the answer – preferably a nice Norwegian one. Harald didn't know many Norwegian birds in Cardiff though, and so decided to take a holiday back to Norway in the summer of 1911. During a trip on a steam ship, Harald met and fell in love with Sofie Magdalene Hesselberg and within the week had asked her to marry him! Just for once, the holiday had been even better than the brochure!

Here comes Roald

An over-the-moon Harald returned home to Cardiff with his new bride. Sofie soon took charge of her new step-children and the house. It wasn't long, though, before the pitter-patter of tiny feet was heard once more (we're talking babies, not rats).

Harald Dahl had some very specific ideas about bringing up babies – even BEFORE they were born! As a collector of beautiful things, he was very keen that all his children should appreciate things of beauty as well. So whenever Sofie became pregnant he would insist on her taking long walks in the countryside and making her gaze at the scenery. He believed that if Sofie spent time gawping at beauty then the baby in her womb would grow up to appreciate such things!

Altogether, Sofie had five children with Harald – four girls (Astri, Alfhild, Else and Asta) and one boy whom they named (yes, it's him!) Roald. As full-blooded Norwegians they pronounced Roald as 'Roo-ahl' without sounding the 'd' at the end.

Producing kids at that rate meant the Family Dahl needed a little more elbow room! But that was no problem, because while Sofie had been busy making babies, Harald had been making money in the Cardiff shipping boom – buckets of the stuff. When Roald was two years old, Harald bought a magnificent country house near the little village of Radyr.

The house was huge by anyone's standards and came complete with its own farm. Workers lived in cottages on the estate itself and tended the farm's shire-horses, cows, pigs, and chickens.

At Christmas 1919, a Dahl family portrait would have looked like this:

Things seemed to be going pretty well for the Dahl family and for young Roald. It didn't last long. Tragedy was waiting just around the corner ready to leap out, shout 'Boo!' and spoil everything. It struck not once but twice, and in the most terrible way. Roald's family suffered two deaths in two months! Here's how Sofie might have broken the sad news to her family back in Norway:

Sofie Dahl,
Cardiff,
Wales,
April 1920

Dearest Family,
I'm afraid you must prepare yourselves for a shock. My heart is broken and my family has been hit by a double tragedy. One day in February, our lovely daughter Astri suddenly began to complain about sharp pains in her stomach. We put her to bed and called the local doctor who immediately suspected appendicitis. Then there came the first of our two terrible disasters! Before the doctor could operate, my precious child had died!

We were all grief-stricken but even

worse was to come. Harald took Astri's death even harder than the rest of us. Soon afterwards he caught a chest infection which developed into dreaded pneumonia. To be honest, when we lost Astri, I think Harald also lost the will to live. He simply faded away and died - I think it was a broken heart that was the real cause. I have lost my eldest child and my husband both within the space of two months!

Some friends have suggested I return with the children to Norway where I know you would all look after us. However, it was my beloved Harald's fondest wish that his children should go to English schools, which he believed were the best in the world. I am determined to stay here *in Britain and carry out Harald's wishes.*

The baby (Harald's last child!) is due in the autumn and I will write again soon to let you know how things are progressing.

With love,

Sofie

Sofie did stay in Britain and had her baby, a girl she called Asta, in the autumn of 1920. It must have been difficult for Sofie to go through all this without her family, but she was obviously made of stern stuff. At least she didn't have to worry about money, because Harald had left the family with pots of it from his shipbroker business.

Harald had died when Roald was only four years old. Sofie never remarried and Roald spent the rest of his life without a father.

Norway

Roald was brought up speaking Norwegian as well as English, like the rest of his family. This came in dead handy every year when the whole Dahl household would decamp from England and trek to Norway for their summer holidays!

The Idiot's Ten Second Guide to . . . Norway

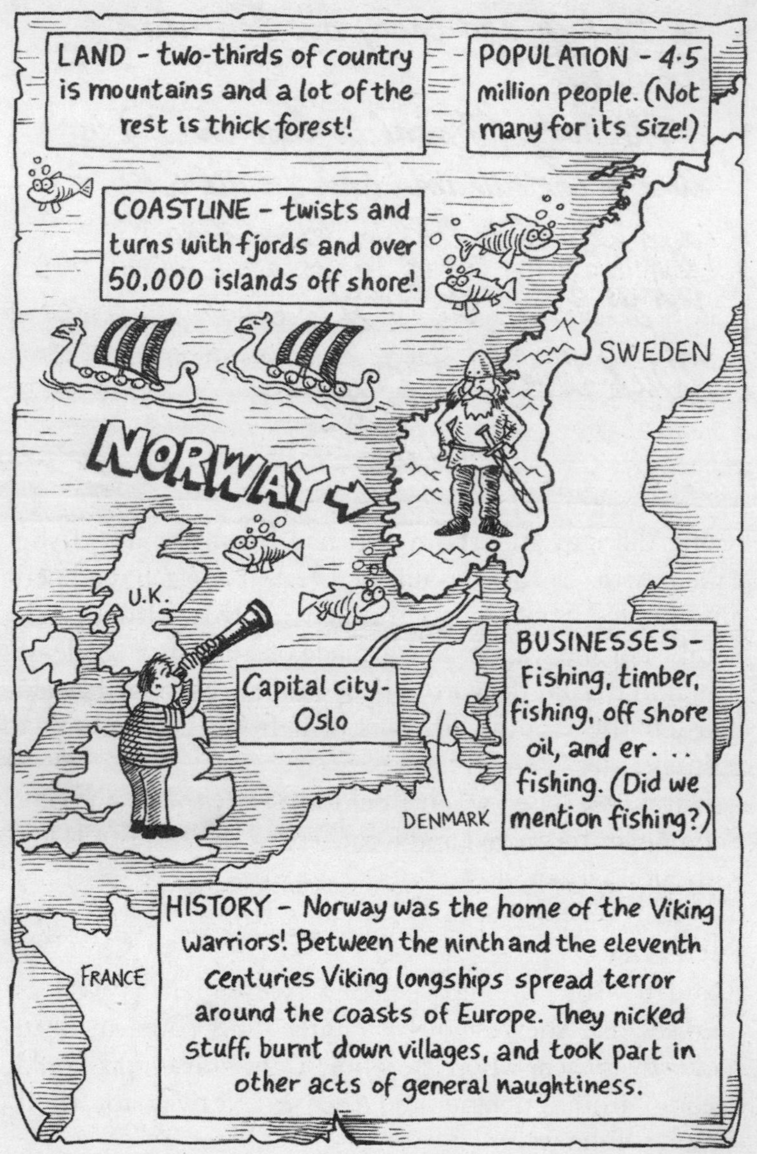

ROALD'S SECRET HOLIDAY DIARY

July 21st 1924. Yippee! The first day of the summer holidays! No school for six weeks and best of all ... our trip to Norway! Every year, our travelling army seems to get a bit larger. This time there are ten of us – that's me, three sisters, one half-sister, one half-brother, two family friends, a nanny and, of course, mother. It'll take four whole days of travelling before we get to Norway.

TO NORWAY

July 24th 1924. Oh dear, the sea crossing was rather rough. Actually, it was very rough. We spent most of it sitting in deck-chairs slowly turning green and trying not to puke! By the time we arrived in Oslo, solid land was a very welcome sight. The first thing we did when we arrived was visit Bestemama (grandma) and Bestepapa (granddad) – mum's parents. As usual, they had an entire feast waiting for our arrival. These Norwegians know how to stuff themselves! My favourite food was the crunchy ice cream with tiny bits of crisp toffee mixed into it. Gorgeous. (I'm sure there's a million pounds to be made by the first man to sell the stuff in Britain!) Tomorrow, we'll head back to the docks and board the steamer that will take us the rest of the way along the Oslo fjord to the island of Tjome and our hotel.

beste-papa
beste-mama
me

August 19th 1924. Aggggg! I can't believe the holiday's over so fast. Every day has been bliss! Every morning I led the dash to our little motor boat. We'd fire up the engine and set off chugging across the water. The fjord was littered with dozens and dozens of islands just waiting to be explored. Some had people living on them. Others were deserted. On one island we found the rotting remains of a wrecked ship on the shore like a great beached

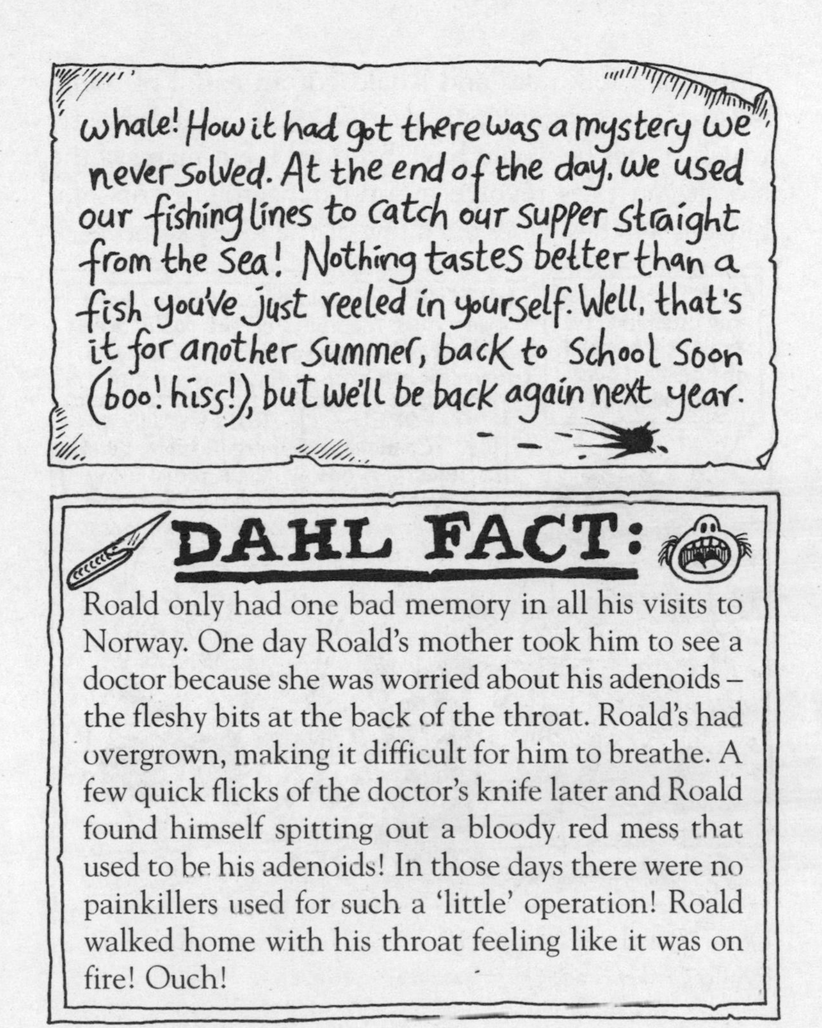

DAHL FACT:

Roald only had one bad memory in all his visits to Norway. One day Roald's mother took him to see a doctor because she was worried about his adenoids – the fleshy bits at the back of the throat. Roald's had overgrown, making it difficult for him to breathe. A few quick flicks of the doctor's knife later and Roald found himself spitting out a bloody red mess that used to be his adenoids! In those days there were no painkillers used for such a 'little' operation! Roald walked home with his throat feeling like it was on fire! Ouch!

Much later in his life, Roald would look back on the holidays in Norway, remembering them as carefree and wonderful times. But apart from the warm memories of boats and islands, did the time in Norway influence Roald in any other ways? What kind of stories would Roald have heard as a boy in Norway? There are loads of

Norwegian folk tales and Roald got an earful of them, mostly from his grandparents. We can't be sure exactly which stories he would have been told, but many of the Norwegian tales revolve around dangerous giants and hideous witches. Here are a few of the likely suspects.

Do any of these suspicious characters look familiar from Roald's own books?

The witch in the sweetshop

When Roald was seven years old, he went to Llandaff Cathedral School about a mile from where he lived. What was little Roald like as a pupil? Was he perfectly behaved? Was he heck! A typical piece of Roald naughtiness happened when Roald and his friends decided to get their revenge on the old woman who ran the local sweetshop. Roald loved his sweets and the local shop stocked just about everything a boy could wish for. The only problem was Mrs Pratchett, the old woman who ran it. Not only was she rude, and hated children, but her hands (which picked out the precious sweets) were always filthy! All the local boys hated her and thought she was a foul old hag.

One day at school, Roald and his friends found the body of a dead mouse hidden under a floorboard. It was too good an opportunity to pass up and soon they'd formed a cunning plan for vengeance. The four boys visited the sweetshop and while one of them distracted the unfriendly old woman, Roald dropped the dead mouse into a jar of gobstoppers. Then they left rather quickly.

The next day on the way to school Roald and his fellow plotters noticed with alarm that the sweetshop was shut. When they got to school they found out why.

The old witch was waiting for them and had persuaded the headmaster to have an identity parade of the entire school so she could find those responsible for the terrible mouse crime! Roald was spotted and later he had to report to the headmaster's office. Corporal punishment was the norm in those days and so Roald received a sound thrashing from the headmaster's cane. Rotten old Mrs Pratchett even got to sit in the room and watch!

The Witches follows the adventures of the hero and his grandmother. They head off to the coast for a holiday, but soon discover that they are sharing a hotel with the Grand High Witch and every single witch in England! Somehow our hero must stop the witches from carrying out their fiendish plan of turning all the children in the country into mice! Things get even trickier when the hero himself is turned into a mouse. (Does the mouse theme remind you of anything?) Roald's witches, in their secret organization, make terrific villains for his book. They are probably the best villains he ever invented – ugly, disgusting, greedy, mean and, above all, just plain evil!

The caning from the dead mouse affair had a more lasting effect than just the red marks on Roald's bottie. During bathtime, Roald's mum saw the damage the headmaster's cane had done to her darling son's backside. She did exactly what Danny's father wants to do in *Danny, Champion of the World* when Danny is beaten. (For more about that book, see page 176.) Danny stops his father interfering, but Roald couldn't stop his mum. Mrs Dahl marched straight round to the school and had a blazing row with the headmaster.

Sofie decided Roald should leave Llandaff Cathedral School. She wanted to send little Roald to a good boarding school in England to save him from any further beatings at the hand (or rather cane) of the headmaster. However, things didn't quite work out that way. Young Roald was about to get a rather nasty shock. Not only was he about to leave home for the first time (sob!) but his new school was going to be a more frightening place than Roald could ever have imagined.

SCHOOLBOY DAHL

Sofie decided to send Roald to St Peter's, a boys' boarding school with about 150 pupils. St Peter's sat on a hill overlooking the seaside town of Weston-super-Mare on the opposite side of the Bristol Channel from Roald's home in Wales. On the first floor of the school were six dormitories – where the boys were supposed to sleep. On the ground floor were six classrooms – where they weren't.

Many of Roald's books feature a kind of undeclared war between adults (usually teachers) and children. The adults make up all the rules to suit themselves. Just like the evil headmistress, Miss Trunchbull, does in Roald's book *Matilda*. The children in Trunchbull's school think of themselves as brave soldiers fighting for their very survival every single day. Looking back, it's pretty certain that Roald's feeling of constant warfare with teachers began during his time at his new school – St Peter's.

Off to school

When the first day of the autumn term arrived, Roald and his mother set off from Cardiff across the sea to Weston-super-Mare. They travelled on one of the regular paddle-steamers that chugged across the bay. Roald was allowed to bring a large trunk for his clothes, and a smaller wooden box called a tuck-box to keep his personal belongings in.

Sofie dropped Roald off at school and, detecting that mothers were not welcome, wisely beat a hasty retreat. As his mother's taxi disappeared through the school gates, Roald started to cry. If he'd known the kind of torture that lay in store, he might have saved his tears for later.

It was the first time Roald had ever been away from his family overnight. And this wasn't just overnight – he wasn't going to see them again for weeks and weeks! How would he survive? When he climbed into bed that night, Roald made sure he went to sleep facing in the direction of home. Not much comfort, but what's a boy to do? Well, actually, quite a lot.

It was no surprise that new boy Roald soon came down with a terrible disease: homesickness. Within a few weeks of the start of term, Roald's devious and cunning brain was working on a way of getting himself shipped back to the bosom of his family. Even if he had to lie to do it.

Roald's marvellous medical scam

In the summer of that year, 1925, Roald's half-sister Ellen had suffered from appendicitis. The whole family must have been especially worried because that's what Astri had died of five years before. Roald recalled waiting anxiously as the doctor had operated on Ellen on the nursery table. (Yes, I know this is all happening less than a hundred years ago and that's really not very long, but doctors really used to arrive at people's houses and perform operations in their own homes.)

The operation was successful and Ellen was fine, but all this had given Roald an idea for escaping from school.

Before he would be sent home, however, Roald had to convince the mountainous Matron that something was really wrong. Thanks to his half-sister, young Roald knew exactly what the symptoms of appendicitis were, AND how to fake them. He let out yelp of pain when the matron touched what he knew was just the right spot on his stomach. Then Roald performed the same scam on the school doctor. It worked. A few hours later, and Roald was on a paddle-steamer heading for home to be reunited with his mother. He was so happy he had to keep reminding himself to look miserable. (Well, he was supposed to be ill!)

Of course the very first thing Mrs Dahl did was to take her sickly son straight to the local quack, Dr Dunbar. It took him about one tenth of a second to spot what the others hadn't – Roald was faking it. If the doctor told the headmaster at St Peter's, then Roald knew he'd be in dead trouble. Luckily for Roald, the doctor took pity on him. He made Roald promise never to fake an illness again. In return, the doc told the school Roald had a stomach infection and would need three days' rest at home. (Perhaps this little adventure sent an early message to the young Roald that you could get away with most things – if you had the nerve.)

Know your enemy – a boy's guide to St Peter's

Despite his best efforts, Roald found himself back at St Peter's a few days later. For Roald to survive he had to know who his friends were. And even more importantly, his enemies. . .

Name: Headmaster.

Job: The Head runs the entire school and lives in a bit of the building with his family – Mrs Headmaster and their two daughters.

Appearance: Tall as a giant. Uses lashings of horrid hair cream.

Dark Secret: Administers fantastically painful punishments in his study using a variety of canes. Canings are usually given in groups of four or six strokes.

Distinguishing Marks: Gold tooth in front of mouth.

Pet Hates: Boys.

Powers: Has absolute control over all small creatures (i.e. boys) in the school. Rules with iron fist in an iron glove.

Danger Rating: 8/10

Name: Matron.

Job: In charge of boys' personal health and happiness (she fails miserably).

Appearance: Frightening bulky woman with a huge bosom which has been known to enter rooms several minutes ahead of the rest of her.

Dark Secret: Is in love with one of the Latin masters, Mr Corrado. (Have been spotted kissing in the matron's room!)

Distinguishing Marks: Large bosom – see above.
Pet Hates: All boys.
Powers: Her word is absolute law in any of the upstairs dormitories. Doubles as Nurse, and on the plus side can admit anyone to the school sickroom for a bit of a rest.
Danger Rating: 8/10

Name: Mr Pople.
Job: School caretaker and handyman. His duties include general repairs as well as ringing the school bell for the start of morning inspection.
Dark Secret: Probably wishes he were a proper master.
Distinguishing Marks: Face as red as a boiled beetroot.
Pet Hates: Boys. (No surprise there, then.)
Powers: Can send any boy of his choice to the Head for punishment.
Danger rating: 7/10

Name: Captain Hardcastle.
Job: Latin master.
Appearance: Skinny-limbed and famous for his greasy, bright orange hair. Served in the army in the First World War and still uses his 'Captain' title like it impresses people.

Dark Secret: Rumoured to have got shell-shock in First World War. Famous in school for twitching and grunting at randomly selected moments.

Distinguishing Marks: Huge curled orange moustache and, of course, his twitch.

Pet Hates: All boys. Has it in for everybody, but especially one R Dahl, who committed the terrible crime of 'looking at me in a funny way in the corridor one morning'.

Powers: Controls destiny of all the boys in his 'care'.

Danger Rating: 9/10 (Note: 10/10 if you're R Dahl).

Name: Mrs O'Connor.

Job: Baby-sitting the older boys (i.e. keeping them out of trouble) while the masters go down the pub.

Appearance: Tall, with flowing grey hair. Appears as if by magic every Saturday morning.

Dark Secret: Most of the older boys are in love with her.

Distinguishing Marks: Excess of bracelets and rings make her resemble a walking jewellery shop.

Pet Hates: None. (Mrs O'Connor is a kind woman – perhaps that's why the school only employs her for two hours a week?)

Powers: Speaks about books in the manner of an enchanting goddess. Marvellous.

Danger rating: 1/10

You might wonder what people like the headmaster and Captain Hardcastle, who seemed to hate schoolboys so much, were doing running a school full of, er . . . schoolboys. It was a question that crossed the minds of Roald and his fellow inmates on more than one occasion.

DAHL FACT:

During the first Christmas holiday from St Peter's Roald very nearly lost his nose! His older half-sister had learned to drive a car for the first time. Perhaps being his half-sister, she'd only half-learned. The whole family were in the car when she managed to crash it into a hedge. Everyone was all right except Roald, whose nose had been nearly sliced off by glass from the windscreen. Ouch! It was up to Dr Dunbar to save the day (and nose) by sewing it back on again. As we'll see later, this wouldn't be Roald's last high speed accident!

Writing home

There were many, many rules at St Peter's. One of them was writing home. Every Sunday before church, each boy had to write a letter to his adoring parents. As the boys all sat in rows scribbling away for all they were worth, the headmaster would slowly patrol the room and watch over the shoulders of each boy and see exactly what was being written.

Roald and the other boys were convinced the headmaster's keen interest went beyond their spelling and grammar. They thought he was spying on them to make sure they didn't write anything bad about his precious school. Maybe they were right.

A typical letter home usually went something like this:

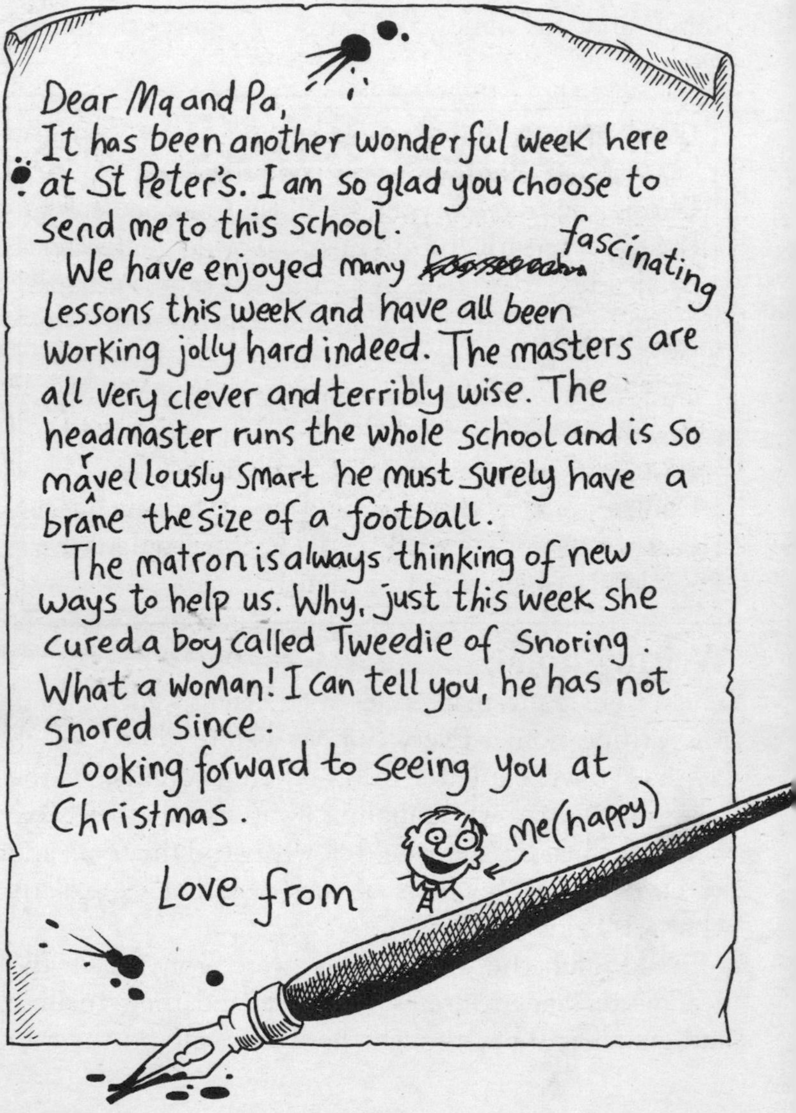

Dear Ma and Pa,

It has been another wonderful week here at St Peter's. I am so glad you choose to send me to this school.

We have enjoyed many fascinating lessons this week and have all been working jolly hard indeed. The masters are all very clever and terribly wise. The headmaster runs the whole school and is so marvellously smart he must surely have a brane the size of a football.

The matron is always thinking of new ways to help us. Why, just this week she cured a boy called Tweedie of snoring. What a woman! I can tell you, he has not snored since.

Looking forward to seeing you at Christmas.

Love from

me (happy)

But the letter the boys probably *wanted* to write went more like this:

Dear Ma and Pa,
It has been another typical week here at St Peter's. I am so sorry you choose to send me to this ~~Schule~~ School.
We have slept through many boring lessons this week and have all been working jolly hard indeed on doing as little as possible. The masters are all very strict and terribly short-tempered. The Headmaster runs the whole school and is so marvellously good at caning that your backside smarts for days afterwards.
Matron is always thinking of new ways to help us. Why, just this week she cured a boy called Tweedie of snoring. She dropped soap flakes into his open mouth while he was asleep. What a woman! He woke up frothing at the mouth and I can tell you he has not snored since. (Actually he's not slept since either!)
Desperately looking forward to seeing you at Christmas
Love from
me (miserable) X X X

By the way, the story about the matron and the soap is true. The Matron thought she had heard boys talking one night, but it turned out to be Tweedie snoring instead. Bet he wished he *had* been talking when he woke up with a mouth full of soap suds! Ugh!

Mr Average

You're probably wondering what our Roald was like as a pupil. Did the future award-winning author show any early signs of his great talent? Did his English teacher stand up and clap every time he handed in an essay? Well actually, no. Rather the opposite.

It's a happy fact of life that many famous and talented people simply fail to shine while at school. Happy, because you can rub it in the face of your least favourite teacher when they have a go at you. Roald was turning out to be a pretty average student in most of his classes. The only thing Roald *did* have a real gift for was mischief. He was beginning to discover his talent for practical jokes. While away on one of the family's regular expeditions to Norway, Roald had invented what he called 'Goats' Tobacco'. Roald's much older half-sister had brought a boyfriend along on the holiday. While the two love birds were away swimming, Roald picked up the boyfriend's pipe and pulled out all the tobacco. Then he substituted a thumbful of delicious goats' droppings in its place. Then he sat back to watch the fun.

Roald's taste for practical jokes – both harmless and cruel – would stay with him for the rest of his life. Here's a typical jape from when he was nine:

Roald's Practical Jokes – Number 25 in a lifetime series: Roald's Big Bomber

7. PULL BACK STRING AS BOMBING MACHINE PASSES OVERHEAD AND SCORE DIRECT HIT!
8. HIDE IN DISTANCE ENJOYING SOUND OF SCREAMING LADIES.
ARRG!
9. WATCH AS LADIES HEAD STRAIGHT TO HOUSE TO COMPLAIN TO MOTHER.
10. DO A RUNNER.
11. HAVE MECCANO SET TAKEN AWAY FOR REST OF HOLIDAY.
Meccano
12. BE QUIETLY PLEASED WITH SELF ANYWAY.

A boy's best things

If someone had asked Roald to make a list of his favourite things (other than practical jokes that is), it would probably have looked something like this:

→ and see where all these funny-named places really are. Also why are foreign stamps more colourful than ours?)

6 Listening to Mrs O'Connor talk about books. (Obvious – see above.)

7 Reading comics (Especially the Dandy and Beano.)

8 Reading books. (Particularly stories of dangerous adventure, war, and exploring unknown and dangerous places where danger might lurk in a dangerous manner.)

9 Listening to Mrs O'Connor talk about books.

10 Listening to Mrs O'Connor talk about anything.

Perhaps the only small clue to his future life as a writer was in his love of reading. He had always loved reading comics like *The Dandy* and *The Beano*. But during his final years at St Peter's, he started reading books like they were going out of fashion. The reason might have had something to do with a certain Mrs O'Connor.

The book goddess

Every Saturday, all the masters of St Peter's left the school for the entire morning. They squeezed themselves into five cars and drove to the local pub – doubtless to recover from the trauma of teaching Roald all week.

The boys remaining behind were left in the care of Mrs O'Connor. It was her job to keep the lads out of mischief while the masters were away getting merry. But for many of the boys, Roald included, she did far more than just keep them out of trouble. Each week Mrs O'Connor gave a talk on English literature. She picked a writer, talked about his life, his works, and read some of his writings aloud. The effect on Roald was electrifying. He soon began to count the seconds until the Saturday morning talk. Roald also began to read everything he could lay his hands on.

Some of his favourite reads were adventure novels by the likes of:

- H Rider Haggard – posh bloke who wrote 34 adventure stories. His two most famous books are *King Solomon's Mines* and *She*. Most of his books were set in exotic locations like the dark continent of Africa.
- Captain Frederick Marryat – ex-naval Captain who wrote many sea stories including *The Phantom Ship*.
- Rudyard Kipling – much-travelled Nobel Prize-winning author of *The Jungle Book*, the *Just So Stories* and many other books.

When Roald was 13, it was time for him to leave St Peter's. While Roald had been in his final years there, his mother and sisters had moved house. They'd finally left Wales for good, and had moved to Bexley, Kent – about half an hour by train from London. Sofie used some of the money her dead hubby Harald had left her to buy a new house, called Oakwood. It had eight bedrooms AND its own tennis court. (Pretty good, huh?)

Roald, meanwhile, had a hand in picking his next school himself. He had the choice between Repton and Marlborough. He chose Repton because it was easier to say. But if Roald had any hopes his next school would be an easier place to live as well then he was to be sadly mistaken. For Roald, it was a case of out of the frying pan and straight into the fire. . .

REPTON

New rules

For a start, the rules at Repton were very different. At St Peter's the Headmaster could cane anyone he wanted. At least that would no longer be Roald's main worry at Repton. Oh no. At Repton, the older boys could cane anyone they wanted. Hang on – schoolboys caning other schoolboys? Surely some mistake? Roald thought so, but those were the rules.

A lot of things were different about his new school. For a start there was the uniform.

Dressing for Repton

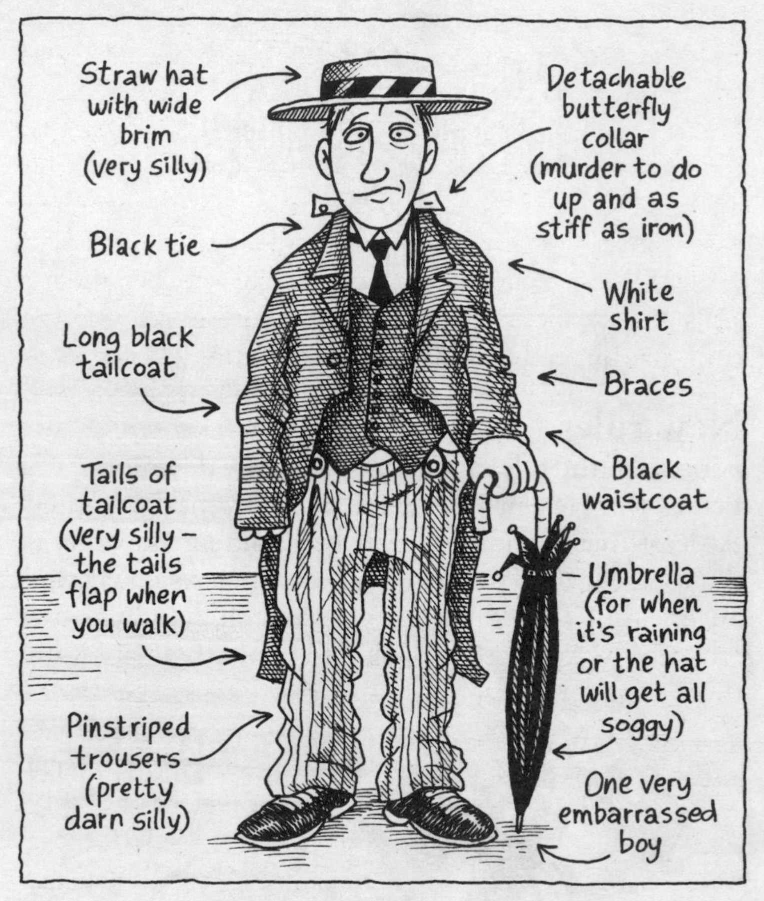

Roald complained that the outfit made him look like he worked in a funeral home.

So what was Repton like?

Repton was located just south of Derby in the Midlands. It was a private boarding school for boys with rather expensive fees.

The most important thing about Repton as far as Roald was concerned was the pain. At Repton, the prefects were known as Beausieurs (pronounced 'Boazers') and could cane any boy in the years below them. The school also had a system of 'fagging'. A fag was a younger boy (13 or 14) who had to do jobs for an older student (17 or 18). In practice, this meant the younger boys were practically slaves for the older ones. They had to light fires, clean floors, even make the Beausieurs' toast at tea time. Any lateness or failure in duty of any kind was severely punished. The canings, sometimes called floggings, were usually given at the end of the day, just before bedtime. (And you thought your school was tough.)

If you were a fag and you heard one of the House Beausieurs shouting out 'faaaaaaaaaaaaaaag!' then you had to run like mad straight to the person calling. The House Beausieurs could order any fag to do anything. Whenever the cry of 'fag!' went up, boys hurtled around like lightning to get there as quickly as they could. Why? Because whichever boy got there last was always chosen to do the job. (While the rest escaped, at least for now.)

Roald spent two years as a fag. He hadn't been a big fan of St Peter's but this was far worse.

Repton was a strange place. Which of the six stories over the page do you think are true – and which are a load of old tosh we made up on the spot?

1. CRIME AND PUNISHMENT

Boys being caned were given the choice between three strokes of the cane with their dressing gown off, or four with it on. (How generous.)

2. GONE WITH THE WIND

Roald's maths teacher used to complain about boys farting in the classroom and used to make them stop work to open all the doors and windows.

3. WELL DONE

Boys were caned for the terrible crime of burning toast at teatime.

4. SNEAKY SNAKE

Roald's teacher once brought a live snake into the class just to avoid having to do any work.

5. THE WARM-UP MAN

Roald was ordered to go and sit on a lavatory seat in the chilly outside loos just to warm it up for an older boy.

6. CROWNING GLORY

Roald's headmaster went on to crown the Queen of England.

Answers:
1 True. Apparently the smart move was always to take four strokes of the cane with the dressing gown firmly ON. The cushion factor more than made up for the extra stroke.
2 True. The teacher's name was Corkers and Roald remembered him as doing anything to avoid teaching maths. (He said maths was deadly dull, and who's to argue with a maths teacher about that?) Every now and again Corkers would call a fart alert. The boys would then open all the windows in the room, and move the door like a giant fan. Corkers would leave the room, blaming the Brussels sprouts in the school dinners.
3 True again. One of the many duties of the fags was making toast for the older boys. In the winter, the younger boys used the open fire in the school library. The problem was there were often too many small boys toasting for everyone to make a good job of it. The boys who served up burnt toast to their elders were in for another caning.
4 True. You might have guessed that it was Corkers, the lazy maths master, who was the teacher responsible for this marvellous time-wasting tactic. Well done, sir!
5 True. (See, Repton really WAS a strange place.) It happened most during Roald's first winter at the school. He was often placed on bog-warming duty by an older boy called Wilberforce. He seemed most impressed with the temperature of Roald's bottie and used him many times as a winter seat warmer.

6 Sounds madly unlikely, I know, but it is true. (Honest!) Roald's first headmaster at Repton did indeed crown the Queen of England! His name was Reverend Geoffrey Fisher and he eventually became the Archbishop of Canterbury. In 1953, he was watched by zillions of peeps around the world as he popped the crown on the head of England's new queen in the middle of Westminster Abbey! (Bet your headmaster has never crowned a royal!)

A good sport

For most of his time at Repton, Roald was rather lonely and felt like an outsider at his own school. He would rather have been back at home with his family. But Roald did find a few things he enjoyed doing. He was good at most sports and played for the school football and hockey teams. The game Roald loved most was Fives – a very fast ball game played by hitting a small ball around a court. The ball is whacked around with a glove worn on the player's hand. Roald won Repton's Fives championship, and was team captain in matches with other schools. In his last year, Roald took up boxing for a short time. With his height and long arms, Roald found it was relatively easy to win the school boxing competition and added it to his list of other sporting triumphs.

Three cheers for chocolate

Roald had always loved chocolate. At Repton something amazing started to happen. He was given chocolate completely free! If you can't imagine the headmaster handing out sweets to the boys – you'd be right. The chocolate bars came direct from Cadbury's – England's biggest chocolate maker. Every so often (not often enough according to the boys) each pupil would be given a cardboard box full of 12 different chocolate bars. Each of them was numbered. Also inside the box was a blank form for the boys to rate the bars for tastiness!

Cadbury's were using the school for free market research – finding out what hungry schoolboys liked to eat. Eleven out of the 12 bars were normally brand new inventions no one had ever tasted. Only a few of the most popular ones ever made it on to the shelves of the world's sweetshops. Roald loved the tasting sessions, and took great care recording exactly what he thought of each new bar.

Roald used to imagine himself working in the factory's inventing room where new and wonderful mouth-watering sweets were made. Every now and then he'd make a terrific new taste discovery and march right in to his boss's office to let him sample it. Naturally this modest little fantasy ended with his boss exclaiming loudly that Roald had just invented the finest new sweet in the whole of the universe if not most of Surrey as well.

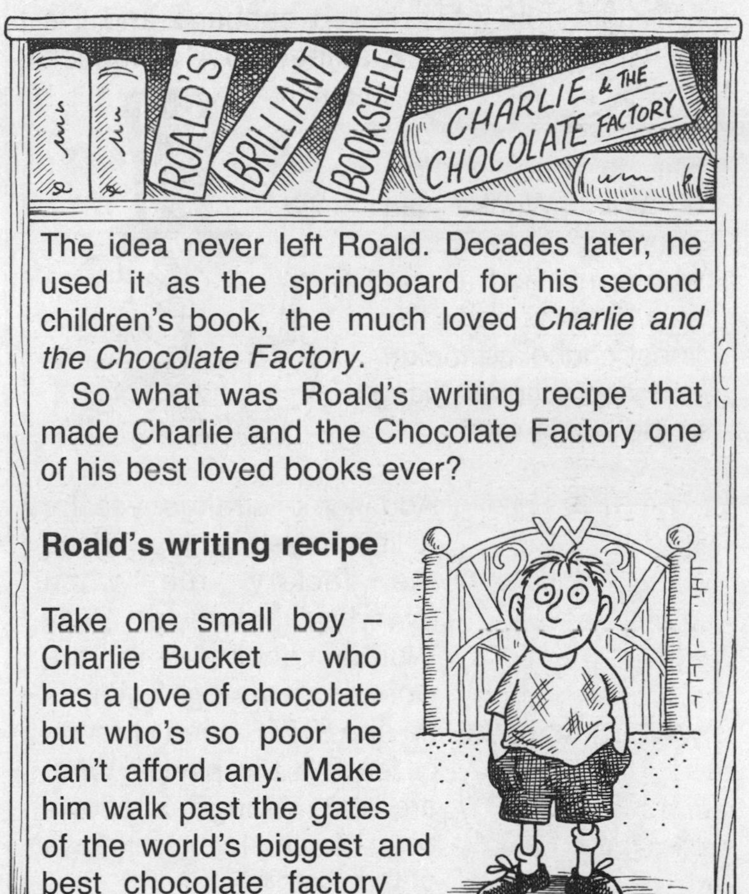

The idea never left Roald. Decades later, he used it as the springboard for his second children's book, the much loved *Charlie and the Chocolate Factory*.

So what was Roald's writing recipe that made Charlie and the Chocolate Factory one of his best loved books ever?

Roald's writing recipe

Take one small boy – Charlie Bucket – who has a love of chocolate but who's so poor he can't afford any. Make him walk past the gates of the world's biggest and best chocolate factory every single day. Let him smell the delicious chocolate but NEVER have any.

Add his parents and mad old grandparents all of whom exist on a diet of boiled cabbage and live cramped up in a wooden shack.

Stir in one portion of Willy Wonka, an amazing, crazy, genius who is not just as mad as a hatter but also the finest chocolate maker and confectionery king in the whole world.

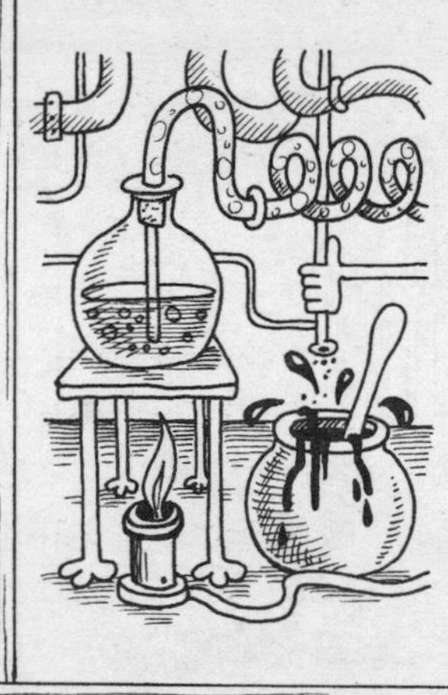

Add some strangeness for a little mystery. How does the factory run when everybody knows Willy Wonka sacked all the workers years ago? Why is no one EVER seen entering or leaving the place? What are the strange shadows seen moving in the windows of the factory?

Lightly simmer by adding a fantastic competition. Mr Wonka has hidden five golden tickets somewhere in all the bars of chocolate that his factory makes. Whoever buys a chocolate bar and finds a golden ticket inside will be given a free tour of the entire factory AND have the chance to learn all Mr Wonka's most special secrets!

Bring to the boil by having Charlie Bucket buy a Wonka's Whipple-Scrumptious Fudgemallow Delight and then discover the very last golden ticket in the competition inside the wrapper!

Allow to boil as Charlie meets the marvellous Willy Wonka himself, a man of great genius, great mystery, great fun, and even greater chocolate.

Roald might have enjoyed the chocolate, but how was he at his school subjects at Repton? If we could take a peek at Roald's school report it might look something like this:

Repton School Report

Pupil: Roald Dahl

English:	Hopeless. Frankly, Dahl has the writing skill of a camel. He is useless at putting his ideas (or anyone else's) down on paper. Suffers from being lazy and is also rather limited in imagination.
Maths:	Average progress. Likely to fart. – M. Corkers.
Photography:	Hides himself away in school darkroom most Sundays. He has produced some good work as he

	showed in the end of year exhibition of his pictures. Everyone agreed it was surprisingly impressive stuff.
Sports:	Dahl proved a big hit this year when he won the annual School boxing Competition. He does well at most sports. He is Captain of the school's Fives team, and also plays for the School's football and hockey teams. A good sport.
Exam Results:	Dahl has been an unimpressive student in most of his classes throughout his time here. To the amazement of his masters, he has (somehow) managed to pass his School certificate in all his eight subjects. Perhaps he is better suited to working under pressure than in the classroom.
General Remarks:	Dahl has a few close friends, but mostly keeps himself to himself. Was in trouble early in year, when he started a fight with another boy he said had insulted Norway. (As if that were a good reason!) Good at sports, but an average pupil in most other ways. We are not holding our breath for great things when he leaves.

Escape

Photography was one of Roald's favourite pastimes at Repton, but during his final months at the school, photography suddenly had to take a back seat when Roald found himself a new love. He bought himself a motorbike! Roald had paid £22 for the second-hand machine and it became his preferred method of escape. Hurtling along country roads at top speed gave Roald a feeling of real freedom for the first time.

Of course, boys were not supposed to have things like dangerous noisy motorbikes at the school. What could he do? Roald rode the bike the 100 miles north from his home in Kent to within a few miles of the school. Then the crafty little weasel found a garage where he could leave (i.e. hide) the bike and walked the rest of the way to school on foot. There were no more Sunday afternoons in the darkroom struggling with negatives after that.

Each week, Roald would walk to the garage and take his bike out for a high-speed spin. Roald told no one about his secret – not even his best friend. He knew that, if he was caught, he'd be severely punished.

Even so, he loved the danger. Every Sunday afternoon he would make a point of driving straight through the village of Repton. His helmet and huge goggles covered most of his face. More than anything, Roald loved riding past people he knew without getting caught. He could fly past them at speed while they had to walk. As with many other things he did, the danger was half the fun.

Roald's time at Repton was nearly finished. Now there was the big question of what to do next. Roald's mother wondered if he would like to go to a swanky university somewhere. There were two things against him going. The first was that Roald himself had other ideas. And the second was that his school told Mrs Dahl he was unlikely to get in anyway. Remember, strange as it seems now, no one at Repton was at all impressed with Roald's brain power.

What Roald really longed for was the excitement of foreign travel. And not just anywhere, but to the deepest, darkest parts of the world. The further away, the better. Perhaps his wish was partly inspired by those exotic adventure stories he'd spent so long reading?

Roald applied for jobs with firms that would give him a good chance of foreign travel – at the company's expense. The company Roald most wanted to work for was the oil company Shell, but neither he nor his teachers expected him to get a job there. He soon discovered that over one hundred school leavers had applied for a mere seven jobs at Shell. This was one occasion, however, when Roald surprised even himself. He landed a job starting a few months later in the autumn of 1934.

Before he started work, though, Roald decided to spend the summer far away, on an expedition to distant and uncharted shores. . .

HIGH ADVENTURE

Roald had joined Shell because he wanted to see the world. There was going to be a rather boring period of training first, however, before they'd agree to post him anywhere exciting. With this in mind, Roald had volunteered for a little summer adventure. He had signed up with the rather grand-sounding British Public Schools Exploring Expedition. What that actually meant was four grown-ups and 50 boys on a giant camping trip to Newfoundland in Canada. Roald was given the title of the group's official photographer. They sailed from Liverpool and began the six-day voyage to Newfoundland.

If Roald had written home during the trip, his letter would probably have gone rather like this:

My Tent,
24th Tree to the Left
Nice bit of Forest,
Newfoundland.
21st August, 1934.

Not sure what this is — sorry.

Dear All:
Here is the report I promised of our adventures. We are well into our 20th day exploring the uncharted parts of Newfoundland.

CANADA
U.S.A.
We are here
LIVERPOOL

It's rather thrilling to think we are the first people to explore this part of the world. Actually it all reminds me a bit of lovely Norway. Our most important task is to collect plant and insect samples to bring back for the Natural History Museum in Blighty. We pick wild berries for food and also hunt for fish.

Everyone carries their tent, food, and equipment in a rucksack on their back. Jolly heavy as well, I can tell you.

I've only had one little problem. I have been accused of mutiny! I always seem to be in trouble with authority figures, wonder why? This time though, it really wasn't my fault. One boy developed a bad case of mumps. I thought he was in no state to continue. However, our glorious leader thought otherwise. He divided up his rucksack between other boys and made him carry on. Things got a bit dicey when I (rather loudly) suggested we should stop.

Anyway, I will be back in England soon. Am looking forward to seeing you all again.

Love from

Roald (The mutineer)

could be berries?

or possibly seagulls?

Roald enjoyed himself on the trip. Physically it was hard going, but at least he was away from Repton.

Mr Businessman

Soon after he returned, he did start work at the London offices of Shell. Roald soon realized he had swapped one kind of uniform for another. Gone was the long black tailcoat and straw hat. In their place, Roald wore the uniform of the businessman. He dressed in a grey suit, wore a trilby hat and carried an umbrella (even when the sun was shining).

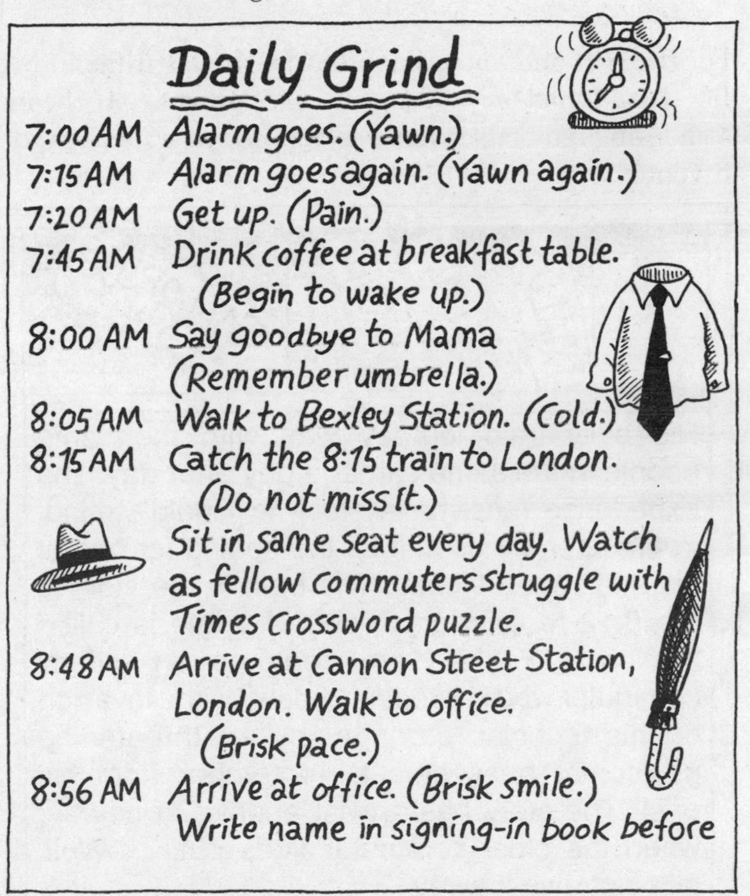

9 o'clock deadline. (Avoid trouble.)

9:01 AM Slip out of rear exit with chums. (Avoid being spotted.) Go straight to café round the corner for fry up of bacon & eggs. (Avoid dripping ketchup on shirt.) oops

For the first and, more importantly, the last time in his life Roald had a proper job. (A 'proper job' being something remotely normal as opposed to writer, spy, or inventor.)

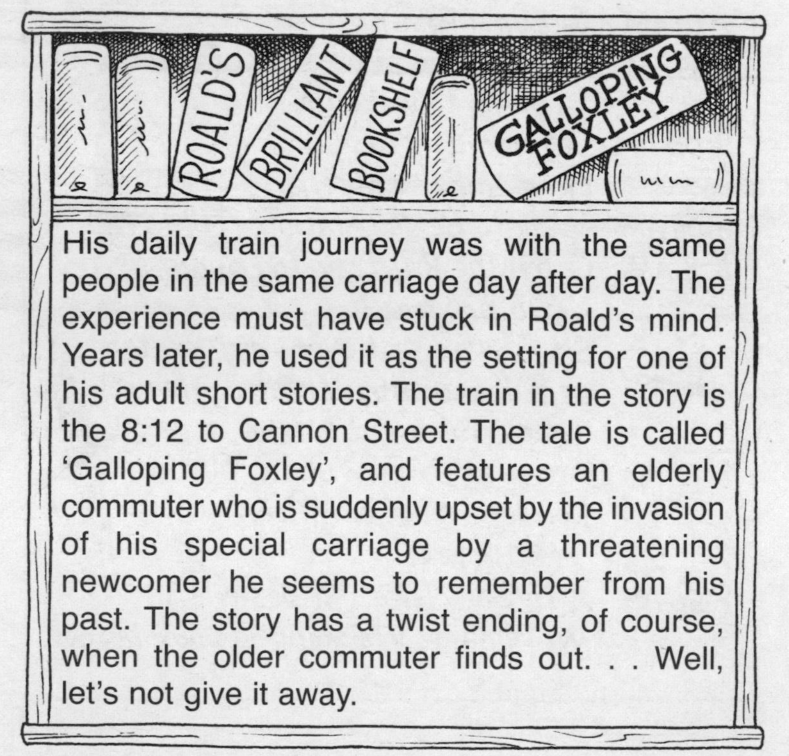

His daily train journey was with the same people in the same carriage day after day. The experience must have stuck in Roald's mind. Years later, he used it as the setting for one of his adult short stories. The train in the story is the 8:12 to Cannon Street. The tale is called 'Galloping Foxley', and features an elderly commuter who is suddenly upset by the invasion of his special carriage by a threatening newcomer he seems to remember from his past. The story has a twist ending, of course, when the older commuter finds out. . . Well, let's not give it away.

Learning the ropes

When he started at Shell, Roald was paid a whopping £130 a year! Life at the London office of Shell soon became a familiar routine. Every day on his way back to the office from lunch, Roald would buy a chocolate bar. Everyday, he would add the silver paper wrapping from the bar to the growing ball sitting on his desk. (Roald kept the ball of silver paper as a souvenir for the rest of his life. We'll meet it once again later – on the desk in his special writing hut.)

Roald watched the ball getting bigger and bigger as he waited for his exciting posting abroad to come through. He had to wait a while yet though. Before Roald would be sent abroad, he was expected to learn about the oil business and the different types of product Shell sold.

Roald spent a year at their Head Office in London before he travelled around learning more about oil and petrol. He spent six months working inside an oil refinery seeing how the various types of petrol were made.

One summer, he was sent down to Somerset to drive a motor tanker. His job was to travel around the small West Country villages selling Shell kerosene from the back of it. Meeting people and driving around in the summer countryside wasn't a bad job at all and Roald rather enjoyed himself.

Finally, during the autumn of 1938, Roald was called back to Head Office in London and offered his first posting abroad, to Egypt in North Africa. It was the thing he'd been waiting and training for for years. Pleased? Excited? Over the moon? Roald was none of these things and less. He rejected it straight away! Why? 'Too dusty,' he explained to his rather puzzled boss. It just wasn't the part of Africa he wanted to go to. Roald wanted jungles and wild animals!

Roald's boss was surprised, but didn't seem to hold it against him. Less than a week later Roald was called in again. This time he was given the posting he'd been hoping for. He was going to East Africa! Roald's 'tour of duty', as it was called, was to be for three years. That's three years without ever coming home even once. When the tour of duty was over, he would return to England and enjoy six months' holiday at full pay (not bad, eh?) as a reward for his travels!

Roald's ship left less than a week later from the docks in London. His family all came to wave him off on his great adventure. In those days, Africa was a lot further away than it is today. Not in miles of course, but in time.

Roald's ship, the *SS Mantola*, would take two weeks to get there. (The same journey today would take seven hours by plane!)

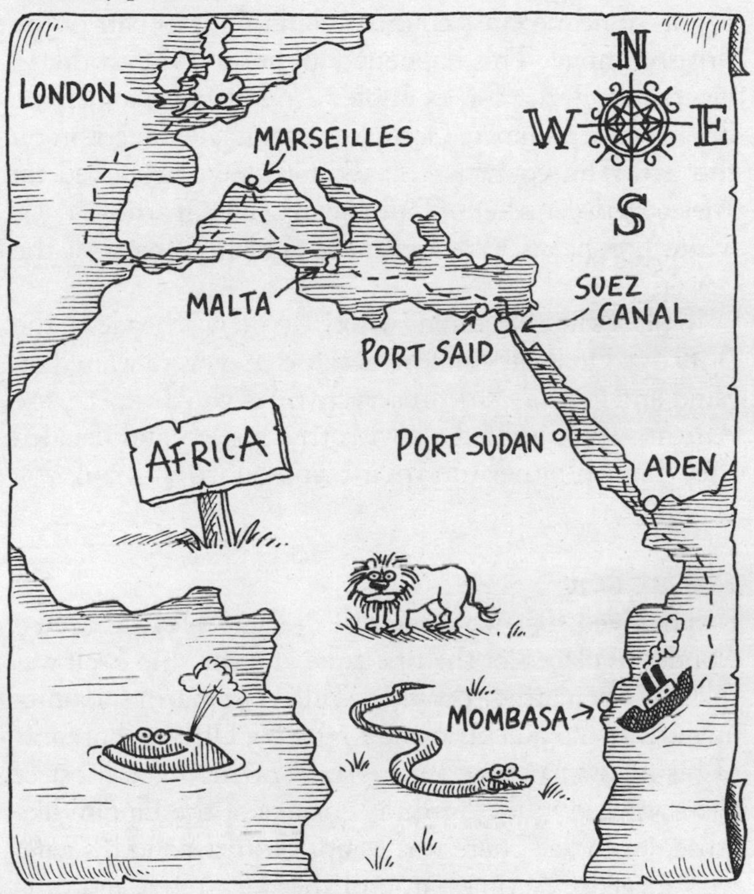

The Age of Empire

Before Roald gets to Africa, perhaps we should say a word or two about the British Empire. Looking back today, it seems strange, but much of black Africa was governed by white people from Europe. For several hundred years before, British explorers had travelled around the world nicking bits of it. What they usually did was turn up with some men, some guns, and stick a flag in someone else's country, claiming it as part of the British Empire. This happened all around the world, in places like India for example. And it wasn't just the British either. France, Germany, even Belgium got in on the act. The countries of Western Europe carved up Africa between them. This meant that, in those days, white Europeans were in charge and held most of the power.

In places like Tanzania (where Roald was headed), the Brits lived in great comfort because they were waited on hand and foot by African servants. As you'd expect, the Africans soon got fed up with this system and decided they'd much rather run their own countries, thank you very much.

All at sea

Roald loved his two-week sea voyage. He was seeing wonderful places for the first time and the ship itself was full of fascinating people. Well, fascinating loonies anyway. Roald quickly came to the conclusion that most of his fellow passengers were stark raving mad. Most of them worked in the far flung corners of the Empire like Africa or India. There was Major Griffiths and his wife, who jogged fifty times around the deck every morning before breakfast. OK, that's not that mad, you might think. Except that they both did it STARK NAKED. Roald watched goggle-eyed through his port-hole. (A port-hole is a window in a ship, by the way, NOT a rude part of your body.)

The rest of the passengers were just as nuts. Miss Trefusis was an old lady who refused to peel oranges with her hands because she said her fingers were covered with too many invisible germs. Roald's own bunkmate, a man with the wonderful name of Mr UN Savory, was three sandwiches short of a picnic as well. Getting ready for dinner one evening, Roald spotted him putting Epsom salts on his own shoulders. Later, during dinner, he brushed it off pretending it was dandruff. This aroused the detective instinct in young Dahl. What was the old fruitcake up to? When Roald returned to their cabin early one night, he discovered the answer. The man was completely bald and was wearing a wig. He put the fake dandruff on his shoulders so absolutely no one would suspect his hair wasn't real. Roald thought he was bonkers, but promised to tell no one about his terrible hairless secret!

Africa at last

When the ship docked at Mombasa in Kenya, a man from Shell came onboard looking for Roald. Now, Roald and all his luggage had to change to a much smaller ship, *The Dumra*, for the last leg of the journey. The next morning, Roald woke in his tiny cabin and had his first eyeful of Dar es Salaam. What he saw must have been pretty close to those dreams of Africa that he'd had sitting at his desk back in grey London. His boat was anchored in a blue lagoon, with a gorgeous sandy beach lined with coconut trees and thick green jungle. Even better, a whole fleet of canoes rushed out to collect Roald and his luggage and take them to the shore. Better than a minicab, eh? Now Roald's African adventure could really begin.

The Brits in Africa all wore khaki shorts, an open shirt, and a topee on their heads. It didn't stop them sweating like pigs but it helped. Roald was the most junior member of a team of three. Between them the trio were responsible for running the Shell business for an area four times as large as the whole of Britain. One of Roald's first jobs was learning to speak the local language, Swahili.

This is Mdisho
- he's like my personal butler.
I have to drive all over the country visiting plantations and places like gold mines, selling them as much Shell oil and petrol as possible.
Here's one of me calling in at a local diamond mine. (Unfortunately, I had to give the diamond back!)
Apart from the swimming, golf and tennis, I spend my spare time admiring the fabulous and er . . . fast moving wildlife.

Like many other people, Roald got malaria while he was out in Africa. Malaria is a horrible disease caught from the bite of a mosquito. Roald's temperature soured to 105.5 degrees and stayed there for three days. His forehead was hot enough to fry an egg.

Snakes alive!

Without a doubt, the most dangerous creatures Roald met in Africa were the snakes. The most feared snake of all was the black mamba – the largest poisonous snake in the whole of Africa. The largest males can grow to five metres long and move faster than a running man!

As Roald drove around in his open-topped car he would often spot a snake, sometimes a mamba, slithering across the road in front of him. His first instinct was always to speed up and crush it under the wheels of his car. He was quickly warned against it. Several people, Roald was told, had already been killed doing just that. Roald wondered how a man in a car could be killed by a snake on foot – well, on belly.

The answer was simple. Most people drove around in open-topped cars, just like Roald. When a car ran over a snake, the snake could get caught up in the wheels. The venomous creature was suddenly flipped high into the air, straight upwards. The snake (now somewhat annoyed to say the least) would then come down and land inside the car, next to the driver! Agggggggg! The thing to do if you saw a snake crossing the road, Roald decided, was to let it cross.

Mamba attack!

One day Roald looked out of the bathroom window in the Shell house and saw a black mamba slithering across the ground. It was heading straight towards one of the servants working outside. The boy had his back to the snake and couldn't see it. Roald leaned out of the window and hollered a loud warning! The boy turned round and saw the snake. As the snake came within striking range, the boy raised his rake and brought it crashing down on to the middle of the snake's back. The prongs went straight through its long body and pinned it to the earth. A stark naked Roald dashed down from the bathroom to try and help. Roald's warning had saved the boy's life.

Snakes were a constant danger, and a few months later, Roald was involved in another adventure. He was walking to a friend's house when he spotted a green mamba sliding in through the open front door ahead of him! Roald rushed to the rear of the house, shouting a warning as loudly as he could. The family quickly climbed down to safety from an upstairs window. The people called a local expert, the 'snake man'. He arrived at the scene carrying an 8-foot-long pole with a rubber fork at one end and a thick sack. Roald watched in terrible fascination as the snake man risked his own life searching for the green mamba inside the house. (Not a job many people would have fancied.) When the snake man found it, the mamba reared up and attacked him but he used the forked pole to trap the snake and bundle it into the bag. Everyone escaped with their lives – everyone except the poor old family dog that is.

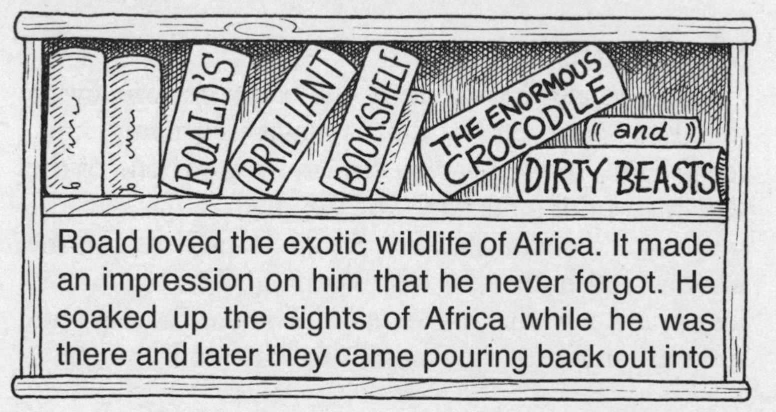

Roald loved the exotic wildlife of Africa. It made an impression on him that he never forgot. He soaked up the sights of Africa while he was there and later they came pouring back out into his books. In *The Enormous Crocodile*, a monster crocodile leaves his river and goes looking for small children to gobble up. The nasty crocodile likes eating children more than fish because he gets bigger helpings. As well as the villainous over-sized croc himself, elephants, monkeys and other jungle beasts roam through its pages too.

Dirty Beasts includes another crocodile, a scorpion, and a hungry lion. At the beginning of *James and the Giant Peach*, James's parents have already been eaten by an angry rhinoceros.

Even when the books aren't actually about African animals, Roald still uses them as similes. A little later in *James and the Giant Peach*, the evil Aunts are described as being like a pair of hunters circling a dead elephant. In *Matilda*, being a pupil at Miss Trunchbull's terrible school is compared to being trapped in a cage with a live cobra. Roald's writing is peppered with references to Africa and its marvellous creatures.

King of the jungle

The snakes in Africa weren't the only danger though. During an evening visit to another friend, Roald was witness to a most amazing incident with a lion. Roald and his hosts were relaxing on the veranda and watching zebras grazing in the distance. One of the servants ran to raise the alarm that something terrible was happening at the rear of the house. They rushed around to find that a large lion had just carried off the cook's wife! Roald's host grabbed his rifle and, together with the cook, they gave chase. The host fired a shot just ahead of the lion. The loud shot made the lion drop the woman from his jaws and leg it for the cover of the thick jungle. When Roald and the others reached her they were amazed to find that she was completely unharmed. The relieved woman explained that when the lion had first picked her up she had pretended to be dead. Pretty good tactics. Its massive teeth hadn't even scratched her skin!

The lion incident was important in another way as well. The story soon became quite well known. By the time Roald arrived back at the Shell house there was a letter from a local newspaper. It asked Roald to write his own eyewitness account of the event and offered to pay him £5 to do it! Roald quickly and keenly got to work. When it appeared in print, the account became Roald's first ever published work! He didn't know it yet, but Roald had just taken his first steps to becoming a famous author!

Roald soon found himself getting a little bored in Africa. He needn't have worried. If it was adventure he was after, he was about to get it. Back in Europe, things were changing fast and NOT for the better.

The Dahly Telegraph

1 September 1939

NAZIS NUDGE NEARER TO WAR!

Evil madman and top loony, Adolf Hitler (leader of Germany's Nazi Party), pushed Europe ever closer to war as he invaded Poland today!

Ever since Germany lost the First World War, national pride

has been dented. Now Herr Hitler seems to have persuaded Germany that they can win a rematch. As the British politician Winston Churchill has been warning, the Germans have spent the last few years stock-piling weapons and building up the size of its armies. It now seems that they intend to use them!

Hitler's troops and tanks swarmed over the Polish border and conquered the country in time for tea. Hitler's moustache was reported to be bristling with pride. Europe feels like a tinderbox waiting to explode and Herr Hitler is the man waving around the lighted match. Britain and France have given Germany two days to withdraw their forces or it's WAR!

Britain and France waited to see if Hitler would take his greedy mitts off Poland. He didn't. It *was* war.

Five hundred million people found themselves facing an uncertain future. All around the world, Brits and Germans who had been living perfectly peacefully together suddenly found that they were living next door to 'the enemy'.

But what about Roald back in Africa? Well, that was about to get very nasty, very quickly.

Dar es Salaam had once belonged to Germany, but they had been made to give it up to the British when they lost World War I. The British, now in charge of the country, decided all the Germans still living there had to be rounded up and put into POW (Prisoner of War) camps. There were very few proper army officers in Dar es Salaam – so guess who got the job?

As a young Brit, Roald found himself given a red armband, a whole platoon of soldiers to order around, and a rather large machine gun. Roald had come to Africa for adventure – now it looked like he was going to get it.

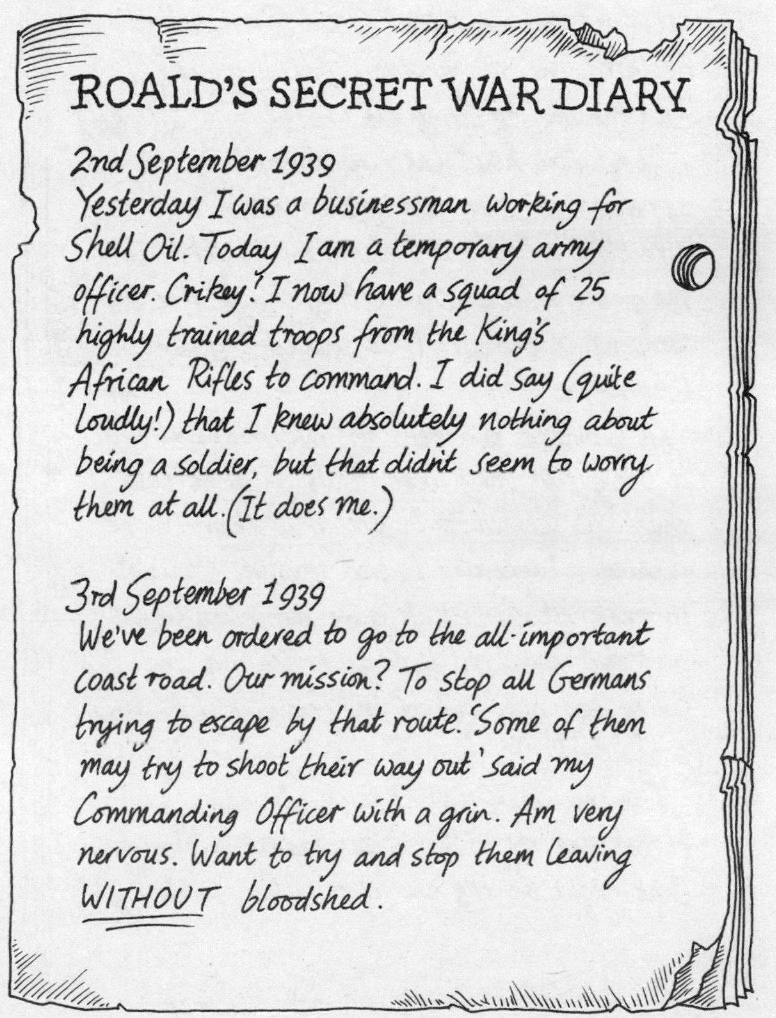
ROALD'S SECRET WAR DIARY

2nd September 1939
Yesterday I was a businessman working for Shell Oil. Today I am a temporary army officer. Crikey! I now have a squad of 25 highly trained troops from the King's African Rifles to command. I did say (quite loudly!) that I knew absolutely nothing about being a soldier, but that didnt seem to worry them at all. (It does me.)

3rd September 1939
We've been ordered to go to the all-important coast road. Our mission? To stop all Germans trying to escape by that route. 'Some of them may try to shoot their way out' said my Commanding Officer with a grin. Am very nervous. Want to try and stop them leaving WITHOUT bloodshed.

4th September 1939
We set up a road block and spent the night camped out under the coconut palms. Next morning, got news that Great Britain had declared war on Germany. Blimey, war! I told the men to stand by.

About two hours later a convoy of cars appeared, snaking along the road in our direction. I told my men that when they see me give the secret signal they should fire their weapons in the air. That should scare the Germans!

As expected, the Germans did not react well to being told they were POWs. A short bald man who seemed to be acting as their leader pointed a large and loaded revolver straight in my chest. GULP! I gave my secret signal and my men fired their guns scaring the living daylights out of the Germans. (And me too actually.)

The leader refused to back off and threatened me with his gun again. I thought that might be the end of me when suddenly there was a 'bang' and one of my men shot him straight through the head. Horrible. Soft grey bits flew everywhere – including all over my shirt. (Though not much blood, surprisingly.) We escorted the rest of the Germans back to town without further trouble.

So this is war.

Roald was always fascinated by the grotesque and it was typical of him to remember the details of the dead man's 'little soft bits of grey stuff' when he told the story over 40 years later in his autobiography, *Going Solo*.

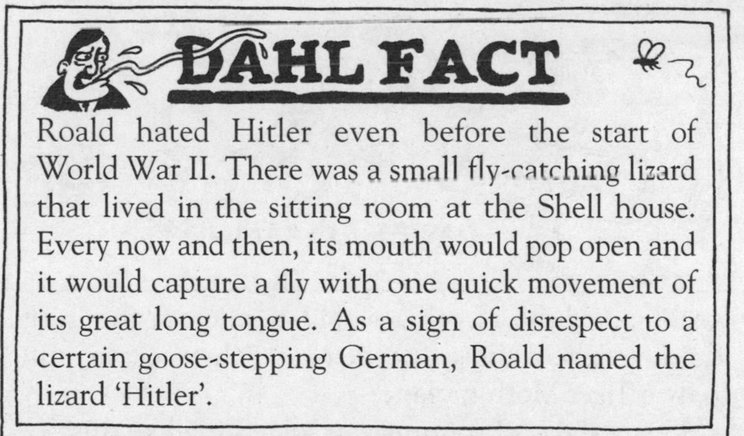

DAHL FACT

Roald hated Hitler even before the start of World War II. There was a small fly-catching lizard that lived in the sitting room at the Shell house. Every now and then, its mouth would pop open and it would capture a fly with one quick movement of its great long tongue. As a sign of disrespect to a certain goose-stepping German, Roald named the lizard 'Hitler'.

Joining up

The world around Roald was changing with frightening speed. As a fit young man, he had to decide quickly what he wanted to do in the war. Roald didn't fancy joining the army and marching around in the terrible African heat. But he had always wanted to learn to fly. Roald soon made enquires about joining the RAF – Britain's Royal Air Force. A complete course of flying lessons would have cost him over £1,000 back in England, but the RAF said they would teach him for nothing. All he had to do afterwards was fly around being shot at by dozens of enemy fighters. A bargain, then! Roald drove north determined to sign up.

Roald joined the 15 other would-be pilots at the Initial Training School and spent the next eight weeks learning to fly a Tiger Moth biplane.

A typical day of training ran something like this:

5:30	Wake up
6:00	Drill (Marching around a bit.)
7:00	Breakfast. (Chance to talk about yesterday's flying.)
7:30	Chase zebras off runway.
8:00-12:30	Fly and attend lectures on flying.
12:30-1:30	Lunch (Chance to talk about the morning's flying.)
1:30-2:30	Flying.
2:30-3:30	More flying.
3:30-6:30	Er... you've guessed it, More flying.
7:00	Supper. (Chance to talk about the day's flying.)
10:00	Bed. (Chance to dream about ... guess what?)

Roald loved every minute of it. His biggest problem was how to squeeze his long legs into the tiny cockpit of his aircraft. He used to have to sit with his knees nearly under his chin and his back hunched over. Roald was so tall that his fellow flyers called him 'Lofty'. Ha-very-ha.

Roald learned lots of useful things like:

That magnificent man in his flying machine

Roald thought he was the luckiest man alive to be learning to fly (for free!) over the Great Rift Valley. Every morning he buzzed over the heads of elephants, lions, rhinos, giraffes, gazelle, and pink flamingos. Roald's flying experiences changed him for ever. He later described every moment as 'totally enthralling'. A few years later, his flying adventures would turn up again in his first collection of short stories called *Over to You*.

In one story, 'Death of an Old, Old Man', Roald describes the feelings of a fighter pilot. In the story, the pilot and his plane combine and move together so perfectly that the man can no longer tell where his body ends and where the machine begins. From the intense way the story is written, that's probably how Roald felt too.

Having learnt to loop-the-loop and all the other basics, Roald was now ready for the advanced training course. The first bit (the nice one) had lasted eight weeks. The next bit (much less nice) was to last six months! Roald and his pilot friends were sent to the RAF base at Habbaniya in Iraq.

Habbaniya was never listed in any tourist books, but if it had been the entry would have read something like: 'Hellhole in the middle of nowhere – avoid.' The base was slap-bang in the centre of a boiling desert and the area around it was full of poisonous scorpions and hostile tribesmen more than happy to take a pot shot at you. Other local delights included regular flooding of a nearby river and the chance to get heat-stroke. Roald's time at Habbaniya ticked by very slowly.

When it was over, Roald was promoted to a Pilot Officer and was finally ready for WAR! (At least that's what they told him.) He was ordered to fly and join his new assignment at 80 Squadron. It should have been a straightforward flight, but unfortunately things went ever so slightly horribly wrong. . .

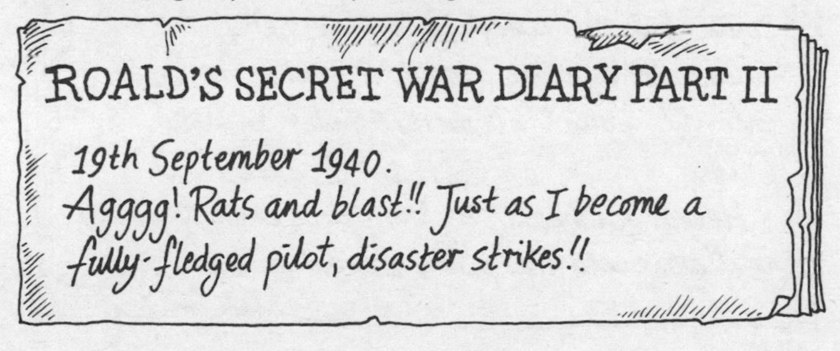

Yesterday I was given the spiffing news that training was over and I was now ready to join 80 Squadron for a piece of the action. Took off in my Gladiator in high spirits and headed towards the Western Desert.

Halfway there I landed at a small RAF airfield to refuel and met the Commanding Officer. He gave me the secret location of 80 Squadron in the desert - apparently they have to move quite often because of German attacks.

About 50 minutes of flying later, I could still see no sign of 80 Squadron. I criss-crossed the entire area searching for them, but found nothing. (Their secret location was turning out to be a bit too secret for my liking.) With my fuel running out and darkness falling I had no choice but to try and land in the rocky desert! I brought the aircraft down as slowly and carefully as I could, but not carefully enough! My undercarriage hit a boulder and I smashed into the ground at over 75 miles an hour. Ouch!

Heard a 'whoosh' as the petrol tank went up in flames and the plane started to burn around me. Heat of the fire started setting off the plane's ammunition! Marvellous! Now my own bullets were exploding and trying to kill me! Mustered the last of my strength and dragged myself from blazing wreckage. Was found in a very sorry state by some British soldiers and rushed to hospital in Egypt.

Feel bally silly – having written off one perfectly good aircraft and very nearly done the same to its fully (and only recently) trained pilot.

Roald was left nursing a series of serious injuries including a missing nose. 'I dust don't dnow where it's gone,' he sniffed.

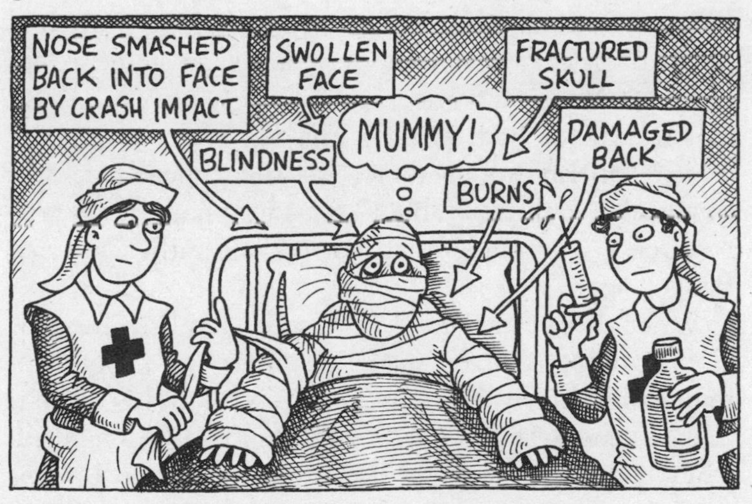

Roald couldn't know it at the time, of course, but his terrible crash would become the raw material for the very first story he would ever write.

It was two months before Roald was well enough to even get out of bed. That might sound like a nice rest, but Roald spent most of the time wondering if his blindness was permanent. (His sight did eventually come back.) He also needed a special operation to rebuild his nose – it was a success, although he sometimes complained that it was still a little bent.

Roald was offered the chance to go home to England, but turned it down. He knew that it would have meant the end of his career as a pilot and more than anything else in the world, Roald wanted to fly again.

Nasty Nazis

While Roald had been busy learning to fly, Hitler's Nazis had been even busier. The Germans had invaded Denmark, Belgium, and France – in fact nearly all of Europe. But that wasn't the only bad news. Italy and Japan had decided to join Germany against the Allies (Britain, America, France, etc).

The Italians had recently invaded Greece, trapping 60,000 British troops there. By the time Roald was finally able to fly again, his 80 Squadron had been posted to Greece to provide air cover for the rather battered British Army.

When Roald arrived ('six months late!' as his new Commanding Officer made a rather rude point of reminding him), he must have wished he hadn't. Because the RAF in Greece were slightly outnumbered. They had 200 aircraft, while the Germans and Italians had over 1,000! It was a bit like playing a football match with 55 men on the other team.

To make things worse, Roald had never even flown in combat before. He soon asked a fellow pilot for advice.

Sounds simple doesn't it? The only problem was that real air battles were so fast and so furious you often had no idea who was actually shooting at you.

After every flight, pilots had to file their official report. RAF reports were supposed to be written in a businesslike and calm style. Roald's however, were rather different. His reports were full of explosions, bullets and danger. He described enemy aircraft bursting into fire and took great delight in detailing the damage he thought he had inflicted on them. No one had spotted it yet, but the writer in Dahl was beginning to flicker into life.

Against the odds

Over the next few weeks, the war in Greece went from bad to worse. British aircraft were shot out of the sky every day. It was a bloody and messy campaign and only a matter of time before the RAF ran out of planes . . . and pilots. Roald flew dozens of missions against the enemy, knowing any one of them could be his last. Sometimes he flew as many as four in a single exhausting day. When he landed he would be soaked with sweat from head to toe with the effort of staying alive. His hands would often shake so badly after a flight that one of the ground crew would have to light his cigarette for him. Fun, eh?

The Dahly Telegraph

25 April 1941

BRITISH SLIP UP IN GREECE

Britain today evacuated its remaining soldiers, aircraft and pilots from Greece in a dangerous and daring operation.

The days before the escape saw some of the most ferocious air combat of the entire Grecian campaign. Heavy German attacks on the capital city of Athens were met by 80 Squadron and 33 Squadron combining to take on the might of the Luftwaffe. 'The German aircraft buzzed over the city like a swarm of angry wasps!' reported one local man. 'Except they were much bigger, weren't black and yellow, and dropped bombs,' he added.

During what became known as the Battle of Athens, the brave boys of the RAF took on German aircraft that out-numbered them ten to one. Five Hurricanes were lost, but ground observers reported the enemy losing 22 Messerschmitts during the same battle.

Despite our brave boys' best efforts, victory in the war in Greece has slipped away from us. Survivors from the Battle of Athens have now been sent to the relative safety of Egypt – leaving our evil enemies with Greece in their grasp . . . for now.

Like most young men who have fought in a war, Roald never forgot it. His experiences would remain with him for the rest of his life. In *Going Solo* he says that taking part in the Battle of Athens was the most breathless and exciting time he had ever lived through.

During the last hectic weeks, Roald had been having worse and worse headaches. They were caused by injuries from his desert crash and meant his career as a pilot was over. Roald was sent straight home to England. Although he never flew again, his part in the war was far from finished. Within a year, Roald would travel to America and become a spy. Even more importantly, he was about to become a writer.

MR DAHL GOES TO WASHINGTON

Roald sailed back to England to be reunited with his waiting family. On the voyage, the troopship carrying Roald home had to survive several attacks from his old friends in the German Air Force – who seemed keen to give Roald a large bomb as a going-away present.

Roald found England was now a very different place from the country he'd left four years before. For a start, there was a war on. Most of the young men he'd known were now wearing a uniform and training to get shot at. Much of the London he'd known had been destroyed in the 'blitz' by those pesky Germans in their diabolical flying machines. Roald's own family had moved from their home in Kent, close to the capital, to a small village further away in Buckinghamshire.

Roald had shot down five enemy aircraft during his combat time – a pretty good score – and, even better, he'd lived to tell the tale. He was rewarded with a promotion to the rank of Flying Officer. Roald was given a period of leave while he waited for his next assignment –

whatever it would be. No one seemed to quite know where he'd be going next.

For the first time in his life, Roald was loaded. He had found there was very little to spend money on in Africa unless you wanted to buy a second-hand zebra. Roald's salary had been piling up in his bank. He now had over £400 – might not sound much, but remember that was in 1941. It would be the same as about £12,000 today! The money soon started to burn a hole in young Roald's pocket. He wanted to spend it on something – something marvellous.

Dahl the collector

Roald found that special something when he came across the paintings of an artist called Matthew Smith. Roald had seen his paintings in posh art galleries in London and soon tracked him down in person. Eventually they became firm friends. Roald was even honoured by having his own portrait painted by Smith.

Seeing Smith's bright and unusual pictures brought out the collector in Roald. Collecting things had been an interest of Roald's since he was a boy and would stay with him all his life.

Here are a few of Roald's collections from different times in his life:

Stamps: Like many small boys, Roald's first collection was an album of stamps from around the world. He asked his mother to send some doubles to his boarding school so he could swap them with his fellow prisoners . . . sorry, pupils.

Birds' Eggs: Young Roald had also been rather expert at collecting birds' eggs. Birds' eggs? Today, only a barkingly crazed madman would think it was a good idea to steal eggs from birds. When Roald was small though, collecting birds' eggs was a very popular hobby. Killing unborn birdies by hollowing out their eggs was considered to be a healthy pastime for a growing lad. To add to his collection, Roald climbed tall trees, crumbling buildings, and sheer cliffs. Total egg tally was a whopping 172. (Not egg-cellent news for the poor birdies.)

Art: Roald didn't know much about art when he met the painter Matthew Smith. He soon learned, though. Famous art names owned and collected by Roald over the years included Picasso and Henry Moore.

Orchids: Roald grew rare and valuable orchids in the greenhouse at Gipsy House. He admired anything that was difficult to do.

Your next mission, Mr Dahl

In a strange way, Roald's interest in art helped get him his next job. A friend took Roald to dinner at a posh men's club in the centre of London. Our boy Dahl found himself sitting next to a very nice chap who just happened to be second in command of the Government's Air Ministry. During the dinner Roald impressed the man with his easy conversation and tales of art collecting.

The man decided dashing Dahl was exactly the kind of war hero Britain needed to send to America.

Why? Well, it was all war politics, really. The Japanese Air Force had just attacked the American base at Pearl Harbour, Hawaii, and so the Americans had finally entered the war. Cue a huge sigh of relief from the British government. The Prime Minister, Winston Churchill, wanted as many men, tanks, and planes from the Americans as possible. It seemed a good idea to have a real live war hero around the British Embassy in Washington DC, the capital of America and home to the President. It was where all the important decisions about the war effort would be made. Being stationed there, Roald could meet people and (with any luck) help persuade them to give more assistance to Blighty.

Roald was given the title of Assistant Air Attaché and told to pack immediately. He didn't have a clue as to what the job actually was, but Roald obeyed orders. He sailed across the Atlantic, taking turns to watch for the periscopes of lurking German U-boats.

Once in Washington DC, Roald quickly realized he was something of a novelty. He was one of only a few people who had seen war action. His tales of dog fights in the skies over Europe were soon much in demand at Washington dinner parties. And being a war hero did Roald no harm at all with the ladies of Washington. The tall, handsome, hero in uniform was never short of a snog or two.

DAHL FACT

One of Roald's unofficial official jobs was to be a kind of spy. Sadly he didn't have any special equipment like a car with hidden machine guns – it was all rather low-key. England and America were batting on the same side of course, but each wanted to know what the other was up to. Part of Roald's job was to become chums with as many important people as he could and keep his ear to the ground.

Something was about to happen that would change Roald's life for ever. Perhaps he might have recorded the events something like this:

ROALD'S SECRET DIARY

– 5th February 1942.

Crikey! Something wonderful and very strange seems to have happened! I can hardly believe it myself!

I was minding my own business, sitting at my desk at the British Embassy, when there was a quiet knock at the door. A tiny man with thick glasses stepped inside, looking like a cross between an insurance salesman and a mole. Then the chap suddenly announced he was CS Forester, the world famous author!

Even better – the great man wanted me to have lunch with him. He wanted to write a story to show the Americans what the war was like. He needed to talk to a real life war hero and he'd picked me!

I tried to tell him about it over lunch, but the food was too delicious to stop eating. So instead, I said I'd write him some notes and send them to him. That night I wrote my notes for Mr F. He had asked for lots of details and I put in as many as I could remember. I rather enjoyed doing it, too.

Just this morning I had the most amazing reply from Mr F himself. He said he had loved the little story I'd sent him so much he had passed it straight on to the magazine. Now they wanted to pay me $1,000 to publish it! How has this happened? I am v. grateful to Mr. F. What a wondrous chap he is!

P.S. Note to self – Hmmmm, $1,000. I wonder if there might be a living to be made in this writing lark?

Suddenly, Roald Dahl was a writer. And not a struggling, penniless writer trying to get into print either. His story was going to appear in the famous magazine *The Saturday Evening Post*, for a fee of $1,000.

Facts and fibs

The story Roald had sold was published under the title of 'Shot Down over Libya'. The tale was presented as fact, but in fact, a lot of the facts were fibs. (If you see what I mean.) What Roald had done was to take different events from his flying days and stick them all together. In his story, Roald crash lands in the desert, just as he did in real life, but it's because he's heroically shot down by enemy aircraft rather than because he got himself lost and ran out of fuel. Just a small difference, then. It was an early example of one of Roald's little fibs. When Roald wrote about his past experiences, he often had the habit of making his own role a just bit more heroic then it really was. Roald did set the record straight later, in his own autobiography *Going Solo*. And anyway, could you really blame Roald for making things a little more dramatic? After all, at the time he thought he was writing notes for a story by someone else.

Dahl in Disneyland

Now he was a published writer, Roald set about his next project – it was called *The Gremlins*. It was the very first children's book that Roald ever wrote and also (in the long run) his least successful. Only 5,000 copies were printed when it first came out. It wasn't available in shops for decades afterwards and original copies are so rare today that they sell for more than £1000!

The large colourful picture book told the story of a race of strange little creatures called Gremlins and Roald's beloved Royal Air Force. Most pilots knew about the legend of the gremlins. The creatures were said to cause the mechanical mishaps in aircraft. If anything went wrong, it was explained as being sabotage by gremlins rather than the fault of the human mechanics at the airfield.

Since it was Roald Dahl's very first children's book, it's worth taking a peek at the story.

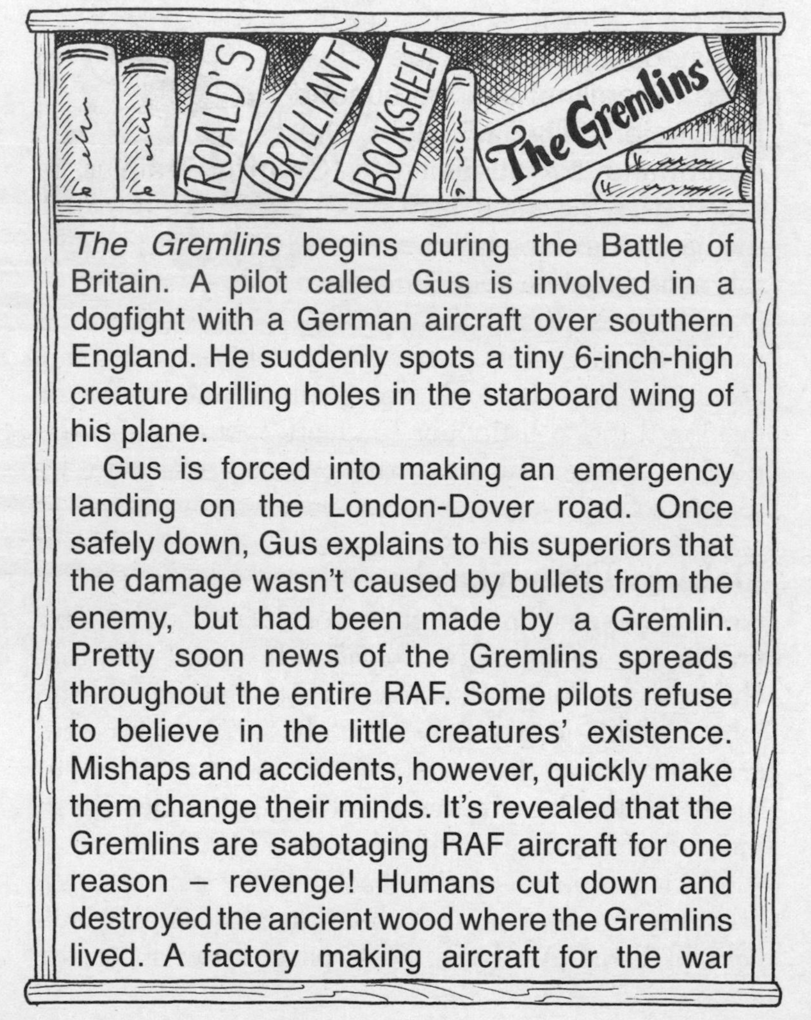

The Gremlins begins during the Battle of Britain. A pilot called Gus is involved in a dogfight with a German aircraft over southern England. He suddenly spots a tiny 6-inch-high creature drilling holes in the starboard wing of his plane.

Gus is forced into making an emergency landing on the London-Dover road. Once safely down, Gus explains to his superiors that the damage wasn't caused by bullets from the enemy, but had been made by a Gremlin. Pretty soon news of the Gremlins spreads throughout the entire RAF. Some pilots refuse to believe in the little creatures' existence. Mishaps and accidents, however, quickly make them change their minds. It's revealed that the Gremlins are sabotaging RAF aircraft for one reason – revenge! Humans cut down and destroyed the ancient wood where the Gremlins lived. A factory making aircraft for the war effort was built in its place, and the Gremlins have been messing up planes ever since. The Gremlins come in many shapes and sizes. The females are called Fifinellas and the babies are Widgets. Their favourite food is postage stamps. In the end the Gremlins are persuaded to help the RAF fight the Germans by attending a Gremlin Training School. The story ends with the Gremlins helping their favourite pilot friend, Gus, to pass a medical exam so he can return to his flying duties.

The story of *The Gremlins* just about hangs together, but the writing is simply not in the same league as that of Roald's later books. In terms of storytelling, it was a step backwards from 'Shot Down over Libya'. Roald hadn't found his real voice quite yet.

Many years later, Roald told another one of his fibs when he claimed to have invented the word gremlins and their legend. Neither was true. Airmen had talked about gremlins since as far back as the 1920s – and by the 1940s the whole of the RAF knew about their supposed existence. It's probably true that Roald was one of the first people to write a story about gremlins, but he certainly didn't invent them.

Because Roald was working at the British Embassy everything he wrote had to be approved by his boss.

Roald sent off his 'Gremlins' manuscript to be checked. Having had one lucky break, Roald was about to get another. Roald's boss enjoyed the story and sent it on to a personal friend of his. The friend's name. . .?

Future children's author Roald Dahl AND the king of children's animation, Walt Disney, working together – sounds like a dream combination, doesn't it? Walt Disney read Roald's manuscript and paid for him to travel out to Hollywood. Roald was given a marvellous car to drive around in and was put up at a swanky hotel. It would have been an exciting trip for anybody, but for Roald, who had stumbled into the writing lark by accident, it must have seemed like a dream come true. It was at first, but sadly it wasn't long before the whole thing went pear-shaped.

The Dahly Telegraph

25 September 1943

GREMLINS FILM SHOT DOWN IN FLAMES

Walt Disney today announced its long awaited film of Roald Dahl's The Gremlins has finally been cancelled.

Hollywood insiders were sworn to secrecy until we

waved a ten dollar bill under their noses. 'The Gremlins got stuck in development hell. The film was going nowhere fast. Even Uncle Walt himself wasn't so keen anymore. But hey, that's Hollywood,' said a source, grabbing the money and breaking into a fast run. It is known that some of the studio's top artists and designers spent months trying to find just the right look for the creatures. They had little success. There were script problems too, as writers prepared different versions of the screenplay, unsure of exactly how to handle the very English project.

The film's cancellation comes as the total amount of money spent on it reached $50,000! That's a lot of money to spend on a film no one's ever going to see! Dahl's original story will appear next year as a Disney picture book. $50,000 down the drain looks like a bad case of Gremlins in the works to us!

Much later, in 1984, a film called *The Gremlins was* made, but it doesn't have anything to do with Roald's story or the RAF.

When Roald's *The Gremlins* finally appeared as a book it did get Roald noticed as a writer. It also got him a very special invitation. . .

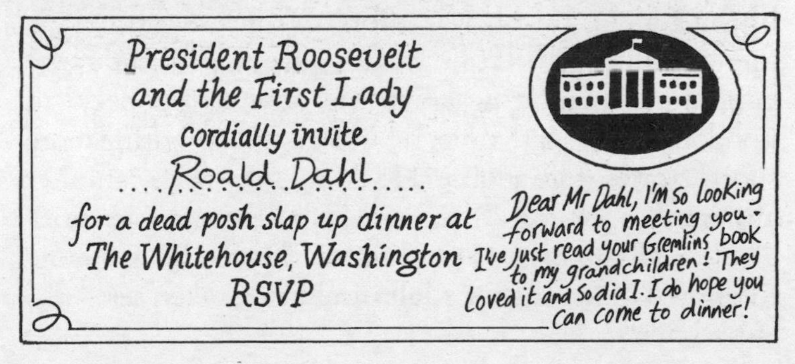

Roald did go to dinner at the White House. He said afterwards he was shaking with excitement as he arrived. Obviously his hosts didn't mind their guests shaking, because Roald soon became a regular visitor, and got to know President Roosevelt and his wife very well.

Roald soon made other famous friends too.

For the next couple of years, Roald continued to enjoy the Washington social scene at the same time as doing his bit for the British war effort. While he was having fun with all those VIPs he was also keeping his ear to the ground and reporting anything interesting back to London. In his spare time, he was also busy writing more short stories for adults. He wouldn't write another children's book for 20 years. Maybe the experience of *The Gremlins* book had put him off. Maybe he was more interested in writing for adults and being taken seriously. Who knows?

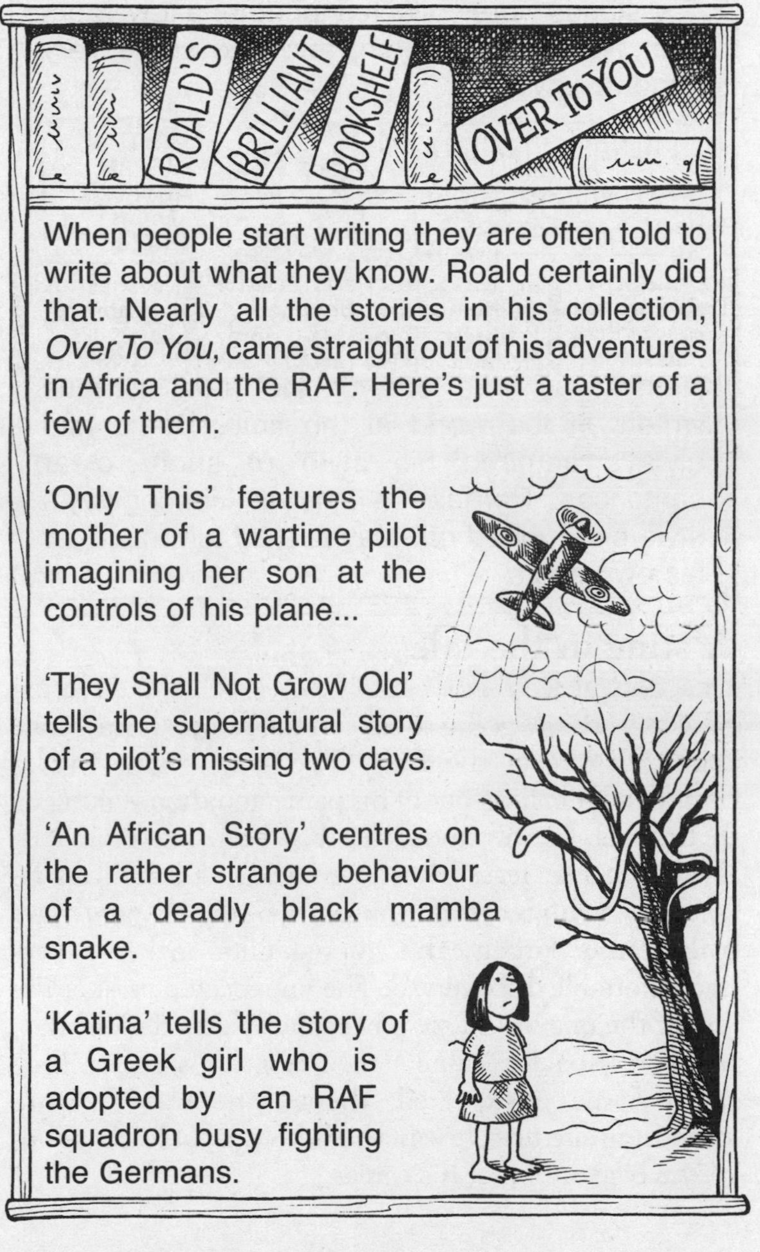

When people start writing they are often told to write about what they know. Roald certainly did that. Nearly all the stories in his collection, *Over To You*, came straight out of his adventures in Africa and the RAF. Here's just a taster of a few of them.

'Only This' features the mother of a wartime pilot imagining her son at the controls of his plane...

'They Shall Not Grow Old' tells the supernatural story of a pilot's missing two days.

'An African Story' centres on the rather strange behaviour of a deadly black mamba snake.

'Katina' tells the story of a Greek girl who is adopted by an RAF squadron busy fighting the Germans.

The stories were collected together a few years after Roald wrote them, and had some very good reviews.

Some people, however, wondered if the writing style wasn't a little close to Ernest Hemingway's. Hemingway was one of the most famous writers in the world at the time. Roald had always admired his style of short, clear sentences. Perhaps a little of Hemingway's style had rubbed off. Maybe a bit too much for his own good.

A sting in the tale

One story at least in *Over to You* showed the direction Roald's work was going to take in the future. It was a tale called 'Beware of the Dog'. The story begins with a Spitfire pilot bailing out of his plane and then waking up in hospital. His wounded leg has been amputated by doctors, but at least he is safe back in Britain. As he recovers, he finds certain things about the hospital don't make sense. Finally, the injured pilot makes a very uncomfortable discovery. . . The unexpected twist at the end of the tale would soon become Roald's trademark.

Before Roald became famous for his spine-chilling tales of the unexpected, though, he was to write something else first. It was a book that would turn out to be the biggest flop of his career.

EARLY WORKS

When the war ended in 1945 so did Roald's job in Washington. He returned to England and went to live in Buckinghamshire where his mother and now-married sisters had moved. Since the war had started just five years before, Roald had found himself doing things he couldn't have imagined. In those five years, he had become a fighter pilot, a war hero, a spy and a published writer.

What next?

Perhaps it was no surprise then that Roald didn't feel like going back to his job at Shell Oil. Sitting behind a desk all day somehow didn't seem as exciting as being shot at or seeing your name on thousands of copies of a book you'd written.

Roald decided he wanted to earn his living as a writer. He now had an agent. No, not a secret agent, but a literary agent called Ann Watkins. Ms Watkins' job was to sell stories and books by the writers she represented to magazines and publishers. Not an easy task when there are always so many people trying to get stories published. Roald decided the quiet Buckinghamshire countryside would be the perfect place to write. He moved into his mother's country cottage and lived there along with her cow, a goat, eight (yes, eight!) dogs, two ferrets, and a large number of ducks. Country life was a bit of a change from the years of swanning around with famous folk in Washington.

Roald's short stories were still selling to magazines, but he wanted to try his hand at something longer – a novel. In the spring and summer of 1946, Roald worked like a demon at his desk, writing his first full length book, a novel called *Some Time Never*. The book reflected Roald's feelings after the war. It was about doom, gloom, and the pointlessness of life. It's important to remember that although Roald was obviously happy about the ending of the war, it was also true that:

- A lot of Europe had been bombed to rubble.
- A lot of people had been bombed to rubble.
- There were still food shortages in many places.
- People were now dead scared of the newfangled nuclear bombs which had ended the war in Japan.

Mr Angry

Although he was trying to knock out his novel at double quick speed, Roald did find time during the summer for one of the things he enjoyed most – a good argument. In April, Roald had read in a newspaper about a farmer who had found a fantastic treasure. Gorden Butcher had been using his tractor to plough a field near Midenhall in Suffolk when he had discovered a hoard of silver dating way back to Roman times. The story brought out the schoolboy lurking in Roald. He jumped in his car and drove the 120 miles to Midenhall to get the details straight from the horse's mouth. Roald called the finished story 'The Midenhall Treasure' and sold it to *The Saturday Evening Post* in America. The editors loved the story BUT – horror of horrors! – they wanted to cut it (i.e. take out some of Roald's precious words) to make it a bit shorter! Not for the last time in his life, Roald sent his publishers a rather stroppy 'Mr Angry' letter. This was the general gist of it:

Dear Sirs:

Yaaboo sucks and a big raspberry to you! How dare you?! How double dare you?!?! Cut my work?? None of my other publishers EVER cuts any words out of my stories. I am utterly outraged, furious, hot under the collar, and just a tiny bit upset you should even think of doing so.

Yours sincerely,
Outraged of Buckinghamshire.
(aka Mr R. Dahl)

A certain editor

This was one of Roald's first angry letters to publishers that we know about. It certainly wasn't the last. Meanwhile, having finished his first novel, *Some Time Never*, Roald set to work on some new short stories. They were beginning to take on the form for which he would become famous. The ingredients of a Dahl short story were:

- Tightly told story.
- Plenty of tension.
- A good dose of gruesome horridness.
- Unexpected (and usually nasty) twist at the end.

Roald sold some stories to the BBC to be read on the radio. After his initial success though, other stories of his were rejected. Roald quickly discovered he didn't like rejection slips any better than the next writer. In fact, given the easy beginning of his career, they probably came as even more of a nasty shock to him. To think there were people who didn't want to buy his work – outrageous!

Some Time Never

After the war there were shortages of nearly everything in Britain: food, clothes, and . . . paper as well. So it was three long years before Roald's novel made it on to the shelves of Blighty's bookshops. When the book finally did appear, Roald probably wished it hadn't. Book reviews at the time were rather like this:

The Dahly Telegraph Book Review

3 October 1948

SOME TIME NEVER FLOPS SOME TIME NOW!

Roald Dahl's first novel *Some Time Never* was branded a huge flop today by every critic in the entire world.

Some Time Never continues the story of the Gremlins, a race of creatures about a foot high who once ruled the world.

Now mankind is in charge of the Earth and they're none too cheery about the situation. The creatures live in a huge system of underground tunnels, only coming out to mess up mankind's bits and bobs. Creatures with names like 'Bogglers', 'Sunts' and 'Snogs' watch as mankind blows itself to bits during another couple of World Wars. In the end, even the Gremlins cease to exist because they are imaginary creatures and there are now no people left alive on earth to imagine them.

Any hopes Mr Dahl may have of being proclaimed a literary genius are ill-founded. One hard working and highly respected critic described the book as 'very disappointing really,' before heading straight back into the pub. Critics and readers alike agreed the book was a strange mixture. Parts of it contained thrilling descriptions of air battles like Mr Dahl's earlier short stories. However, other parts about little creatures with unlikely names seem aimed more at children than his adult audience. We suggest Mr Dahl returns to what he's good at and bangs out some more smashing short stories.

The critics weren't the only ones keen to forget about *Some Time Never*. Years later, Roald would practically rewrite history so it sounded like *Some Time Never* had never been written! When Roald's book *My Uncle Osward* was released in 1979, Roald AND his publisher made a point of telling everyone it was his first novel aimed for adults. It wasn't. *Some Time Never* is one of the very few books by Roald Dahl that you won't find in any library or bookshop.

In *Some Time Never* the Gremlins' favourite food has changed from postage stamps to snozzberries. The sound of the name must have stuck with Roald – 40 years later his Big Friendly Giant had to suffer eating snozzcumbers. (Maggotwise and foulsome tasting things that they were.)

Back to America

Roald suddenly seemed to be having more luck selling his stories in America than in England. Magazines in the USA paid him about $2,000 for each story – worth about $12,000 today. It must have felt like the Americans appreciated him more than his fellow Englishmen (the ungrateful blighters!). Roald was also becoming just a bit bored by life in the English countryside. Maybe he longed for the days of swanky cocktail parties back in Washington during the war.

Roald made plans and returned to America, this time to New York. The reason he chose to go to The City that Never Sleeps (but does sometimes have a nap in the middle of the afternoon) was that Roald's great chum Charles Marsh lived there. Charles was an extremely, marvellously and fantastically rich man. He'd made his money by selling the sticky black stuff that his oil wells produced, and he also owned property and a string of newspapers. Roald had first met the multimillionaire during his posting in Washington and the two had become firm friends. Marsh was much older than Roald and was a kind of father figure for him. Kindly Mr Marsh invested $10,000 into a forestry company owned by the

Dahl family in Norway, and he also set up a $25,000 trust for Roald – so you can see he was a pretty good bloke to be chums with. Anyway, Marsh said Roald could come and stay at his dead posh house in New York. So Roald packed a suitcase and caught the next boat to America.

Dahl at work

In the years around 1950, Roald's short story output was often about two stories a year. That might not sound like very much, but every paragraph – and every sentence – was carefully crafted on his green writing board. Then it was rewritten and rewritten until Roald was happy with it. No wonder he was so touchy when editors wanted to cut things. The magazines Roald sold his stories to paid so well he only really needed to sell two stories a year. It was just as well. Roald told people it sometimes took him a month of work just to write the first page of a new story! His writing diary might have looked a bit like this:

ROALD'S SECRET WRITING DIARY

Monday –

Worked all day. Started a new story. It's called 'The Man from the West'. Had good afternoon's work getting 200 words down.

-Tuesday-
Worked all day. Re-read opening of story and decided it needed a better beginning. Something that will really grip the reader. Rewrote 200 words. Changed title to 'The Man from the North'.

Wednesday-
Worked all day. Crossed out half of yesterday's work and retitled story 'The Man from the West.'

Thursday-
Worked all day. Wrote 300 words then rubbed out 250 of them. Reworked opening sentence. Then crossed it out. Changed title to 'The Man from the South'.

As you can see, it was all very hard work and Roald took it very seriously. He knew being a writer meant spending lots of his time alone, er . . . writing. Not all of his time though. Roald always had lots of friends in New York and he was about to meet someone rather marvellous. . .

Neal Family Productions Present
PATRICIA NEAL
Age: 25
(10 years younger
than Roald.)
Born: Kentucky, USA.
Gorgeous? Just a bit.
Career: Wanted to
become actress from
early age. Has appeared
in Broadway plays and in
Hollywood films.
Is considered to be a
rising star in both theatre
and films.
Most Famous For: Her
long and not-very-secret-
at-all affair with top star
Gary Cooper. The affair
ended a while ago.
The Future: More star
parts and maybe even
an Oscar (for the film
Hud in 1964). And
maybe, just maybe a
husband. Hmmm . . .
now I wonder who that's
going to be?
GORT

When Roald met Pat

Roald met Patricia Neal for the very first time at a posh dinner party in New York. Was it love at first sight? Hardly. Roald tried the top pulling technique of completely ignoring her for the entire evening. It worked. Well, it kind of worked. If Patricia had kept a diary at the time here's how she might have recorded their first meeting:

Patricia Neal's Secret Diary ~ New York

20th October 1952
Dear Diary, Went to a dinner party and was seated next to the rudest man in the world! His name was Roald Dahl. He ignored me throughout the entire dinner. He didn't say one word to me, talked non-stop to the man opposite, and ignored me when I did try to join in. Grrrr! He is a terrible man and I hate him.

21st October 1952
Dear Diary, Cannot believe the cheek of that man. Today the telephone rang and it was that terrible Englishman from the dinner party. Would I like to have dinner with him, just the two of us?! I told him NO! He may be tall and handsome (and maybe a bit dashing as well), but

I never want to see him again. (And that is final.)

22nd October 1952
Dear Diary, That tall, handsome (and a bit dashing) Dahl man rang again. He asked me to dinner at a little Italian place he knows. I was very firm and uncompromising and said, er... yes. Must dash now, or I will be late for our date. I hope he speaks to me this time or the conversation will be rather one-sided!

R.D. P.N.

DAHL FACT

Pat didn't know at the time, but Roald had recorded the exact moment of their meeting – 6:45 p.m. on 20th October 1952 – in his pocket diary. Years later he had that single page framed. It was displayed in their home as a special and rather romantic memento of their first meeting. Bless.

Roald did speak to Pat that night. In fact, he had his charm engine cranked up into overdrive. The couple were soon dating regularly. Pat was acting in a Broadway play and Roald often picked her up for a late supper after the performance had ended.

Things were going well with Roald's writing as well. A powerful American publisher called Alfred Knopf had asked to publish a collection of Roald's recent short stories. Knopf had read a story of Roald's called 'Taste' and instantly decided Roald should write a book for him. The collection was to be called *Someone Like You* and would be published in the autumn of 1953.

Meanwhile things between Roald and Pat were moving pretty quickly. . .

The Dahly Telegraph

2 July 1953

CELEBRATIES SIZZLE IN SUMMER WEDDING SCORCHER!

Actress Patricia Neal and up-and-coming author Roald Dahl tied the knot today as summer temperatures in the Big Apple went through the roof.

The celebrity pair were married in a small chapel in Trinity Church, Manhattan, joined by a select group of close friends. The temperature was so scorching, sources close to the groom revealed, that he had ripped the lining out of his brand new wedding suit just to make it a bit cooler! The blushing bride meanwhile looked lovely in a wedding dress made of pink chiffon. Multimillionaire oil tycoon Charles Marsh acted as Mr Dahl's best man.

After the service and traditional rice throwing, Mr and Mrs Dahl were joined by 70 guests for a wedding reception hosted by Charles Marsh. The happy couple have now left America for a honeymoon tour of Europe.

The honeymooners

Roald's honeymoon nearly ended before it had begun. During a boat trip off the coast of Italy, Pat went paddling in the ocean and was stung by a poisonous sea creature! The guide on the boat cut open her toe with his knife (ouch!) and told Roald to suck out the poison himself. Always good in a crisis, Roald rose to the occasion and saved his new bride's life. (Just as well, the hotels had been booked in advance.)

Never one to do things by halves, Roald had worked out a honeymoon route which would take them through Italy, the mountains of Switzerland and right across France on what was turning into one of the longest honeymoons in history. The last stop was to be England and the village of Great Missenden.

In the village, the entire Dahl family were gathered together waiting to meet the film star bride who was their new recruit. The family hadn't been able to travel over to the wedding, and were anxious to meet the girl that bachelor boy Roald had picked for himself. The newly weds arrived and Roald introduced Pat to everyone before they sat down to a big family feast.

The Dahl family had been growing during the years Roald had been away at war and in America. Most of his sisters were married now, some with children of their own. After dinner the family put on a kind of show, where every member did an act or a little performance. The party piece performed by Roald's brother-in-law, Leslie, was something of a surprise for the new family member.

Pat went down a storm with nearly all of Roald's family, but it wasn't such a smooth ride when he met hers later that year.

The rudest man in the world!

Pat's mother and father hadn't been at the New York wedding and Roald didn't meet them until that Christmas. When he did, Roald showed another side of himself that sometimes came out – Rude Roald. During the first few hours of their visit, Roald decided Pat's parents were two of the most boring people who had ever been born. They weren't interested in any of the many things like art, books, or wine that he was. After that Rude Roald spent most of the visit hiding in the guest bedroom reading books. He only came out at meal times and even then he made very little effort to get on with them. By the time he left, they were glad to see the back of him.

Being rude to people was something Roald did quite often. Oh sure, he could be utterly charming and all smooth and hunky when he put his mind to it. But there was another side to him that quite enjoyed upsetting or embarrassing people. In Washington and New York he was famous for doing it at dinner parties. You could never tell whose nose he was going to bite off next. One reason Roald was rude was probably to get noticed – he certainly did that. Another reason was that at least it stopped a dinner party being boring.

Roald loved being around rich and famous people, but he did have friends who weren't either rich or famous. He liked people whom he considered (in his infinite wisdom, obviously) to be interesting. They might be rich, they might be poor, but they HAD to be sparky. In people, Roald looked for the same qualities he later gave to Danny's father in his book *Danny the Champion of the World*. In Roald's eyes, Pat's parents just weren't interesting so he simply ignored them as much as he could. If being rude had been an event at the Olympic Games, Roald could have brought home the gold medal for England!

SUCCESS AT LAST

Something very important was about to happen to Roald the writer. His book, *Someone Like You* was to turn him into a huge success.

When Roald and Pat finally returned to New York from their lengthy honeymoon they had to buy somewhere to live together. Their separate flats were both too small and so they bought an apartment in a gothic building overlooking the American Museum of Natural History. It had an extra room Roald could have as his work den. A few weeks after their return, *Someone Like You* was published.

The book was a collection of some of the best short stories he had written in the last decade. It included some of the most famous stories

Roald ever wrote. Here's a flavour of the collection (without giving away any of the nasty surprise endings of course).

'Taste' – A man bets his daughter's hand in marriage that a boastful wine expert cannot correctly guess the name of a rare wine. This was the story that made Alfred Knopf ask for the collection in the first place.

'Lamb to the Slaughter' – A woman tries to out-think two detectives and get away with the perfect murder. The idea was suggested to Roald by the creator of James Bond, Ian Fleming. Roald later turned this famous story into a TV drama for director Alfred Hitchcock.

'The Man From the South' – A mysterious stranger makes a bet with a young man that his lighter will not light ten times running. The stranger bets his car against the little finger on the young man's left hand, which will be chopped off if he loses! This is one of Roald's most famous adult tales and has been adapted for TV several times.

'Galloping Foxley' – this was the story inspired by Roald's daily train journey to his London office when he was at Shell. It's about a commuter who recognizes a bully from his school days travelling on his train to work.

'Dip in the Pool' – details the cunning plan of one passenger on an ocean liner to win a pot of money.

'Skin' – is the sinister tale of a penniless old man who owns a priceless painting.

'Poison' – a man is trapped in his bed by a deadly venomous snake that is asleep on the poor man's stomach.

The sweet smell of success

The reaction to *Someone Like You* was excellent. Everyone loved it – both readers and critics. The book was a bestseller and was reprinted several times in just a few months. It was also translated into loads of other languages and published around the world, including Roald's native Norway – which made him really happy and gave his relatives there the chance to show off a bit. Roald loved the attention the book's success brought him. It must have seemed to Roald like he had finally arrived and at last made it as a writer. On the back of the book's success he could expect fame and fortune.

His publishing company arranged for Roald to be interviewed by newspapers and radio stations. Roald adored it. He was always very happy to listen to the sound of his own voice. He also travelled around America doing signing sessions in bookshops where he'd autograph copies of the book as people queued up to meet him. The fact that he was married to a famous film star made the press even keener to write about him and to review his fab new book. Suddenly, Roald was having a ball. In April 1954, things got even better when the book won a major award from the rather grand sounding Mystery Writers of America.

It wasn't all plain sailing between Roald and his new wife though. About eight months after they were married, Roald suddenly turned around one day and told Pat that he thought they should get divorced! Their super-rich pal Charles Marsh stepped in and acted as a kind of referee. He suggested they could (and should) both try harder to make their marriage work. They did.

Roald and Pat had the flat in New York, but Roald wanted a house in England as well – a home near the rest of the Dahls, where he and Pat could escape to the English countryside. They soon found it. A house called 'Little Whitefield' was being sold by auction in the local pub. Their bid of £4,250 got the house. In a few years it would become Roald's only home, and he would live there until he died. A few years later, they gave the building a new name – 'Gipsy House', as it had originally been called in the house's deeds.

GIPSY HOUSE
GIPSY HOUSE - THE FARMHOUSE WAS BUILT AROUND 1800. BEFORE ROALD MOVED IN HE HAD BUILDERS MAKE ALL THE DOORS TALLER SO HE WOULDN'T BANG HIS HEAD ON THE FRAMES.
EXTRA SPACE - THERE WERE EXTRA ANNEXES BUILT ON BOTH SIDES OF THE HOUSE TO MAKE MORE ROOM INSIDE.
GIPSY CARAVAN - SITTING IN THE GROUNDS OF THE HOUSE. BOUGHT AND RESTORED BY ROALD AND OTHERS. THIS WAS THE INSPIRATION FOR DANNY AND HIS DAD'S HOME IN *DANNY THE CHAMPION OF THE WORLD*.
GARDEN - FIVE ACRES OF GARDEN INCLUDING FRUIT TREES. ROALD PLANTED OVER 100 DIFFERENT KINDS OF ROSES.

GREENHOUSE - HOME TO ROALD'S COLLECTION OF PRIZE ORCHIDS.
THE WRITING SHED - TUCKED BEHIND THE GREENHOUSE IS A DUSTY OLD GAR-DEN SHED. ROALD CONVERTED IT INTO HIS SECRET HIDEAWAY FOR WRITING. LOTS MORE ON HIS WRITING SHED LATER.
AVIARY - A BIRDHOUSE FOR A SMALL FLOCK OF PINK & YELLOW PARAKEETS.
VEGETABLE PATCH - WITH ROALD'S FAVE VEG, ONIONS.
INDOOR SWIMMING POOL - NOT ALWAYS FULL OF WATER. SOMETIMES FULL OF ANTIQUE FUR-NITURE ROALD BOUGHT TO DO UP.

Roald was writing new stories, and finding them as much hard work as ever. Someone had the bright idea that he should turn three of his best stories into a single stage play. Doh! It wasn't a good idea. In fact, it was a terrible idea. The play was called *The Honeys* and involved two twin brothers whose wives want to murder them. The plot used different bits of some of Roald's short stories, but while the ideas worked nicely by themselves, combined together they were a mess. Writing-wise, it wasn't one of Roald's finer moments.

New arrivals

Roald and Pat both wanted children. To have babies had been one of the main reasons Pat had married our hero in the first place. On 20th April, 1955, the Dahls were able to announce a happy event:

The new baby's middle name of 'Twenty' came from the fact that she was born on the 20th of the month, AND that Roald was on tour with his doomed play and was receiving exactly twenty dollars a day in expenses. How would you like to be named after how much money your dad earned? After Olivia was born, the Dahls wasted no time in adding to the family. A second daughter, called Tessa, was born in Oxford, England in April 1957. Pat and Roald were obviously keen on kids. Only a couple of years later, their third child – a son called Theo – was born.

Now Roald had kids of his own you might have thought he'd be all grown-up. No chance. His love of practical jokes was as strong as ever.

Another of Roald's favourite tricks was to hang a couple of worthless paintings he'd knocked up himself among his collection of very valuable ones. Then he would listen as his own paintings were admired by so-called art experts along with the rest of his collection. Roald loved playing jokes that exposed people who pretended to know more than they really did. He liked embarrassing adults in real life, just like he did in his stories.

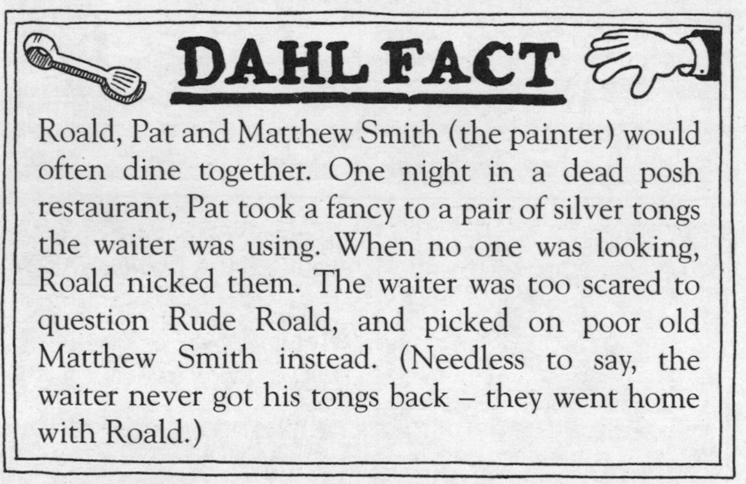

DAHL FACT

Roald, Pat and Matthew Smith (the painter) would often dine together. One night in a dead posh restaurant, Pat took a fancy to a pair of silver tongs the waiter was using. When no one was looking, Roald nicked them. The waiter was too scared to question Rude Roald, and picked on poor old Matthew Smith instead. (Needless to say, the waiter never got his tongs back – they went home with Roald.)

Back at the writing board

While Pat was busy being pregnant, Roald was slaving away at his writing board. It wasn't easy. He was finding that stories were getting harder to write and taking longer. Now that *Someone Like You* had been a big success, he had a reputation to live up to. Roald worked hard and long hours. When Pat was away acting in a play or film, he would sometimes toil away until midnight. Roald himself estimated that one story took him five months' full-time work to finish. That's about 600 hours on one story! No wonder, then, that in the last six years Roald had only managed to produce 11 short stories.

Of course, other things – like marriage, becoming a father and writing a play – had taken time. It also didn't help that the stories were often rejected by magazines! Despite his book having been a bestseller, the editors of a posh publication called *The New Yorker* threw out seven stories that Roald tried to sell them. However, the main problem with his writing was that Roald was finding it harder and harder to come up with new ideas. The stories he wrote needed a strong plot with a good twist at the end. Having written over thirty short stories already, he was now having trouble inventing new ones.

The eleven fresh stories he did have, however, went into a new collection called *Kiss Kiss*. If anything the stories were even stranger and weirder than those in his last book. Here's a small taster. . .

'The Landlady' – tells the story of young Billy Weaver, a salesman, who books himself into a bed and breakfast boarding house only to find that the harmless old lady running it is anything but harmless.

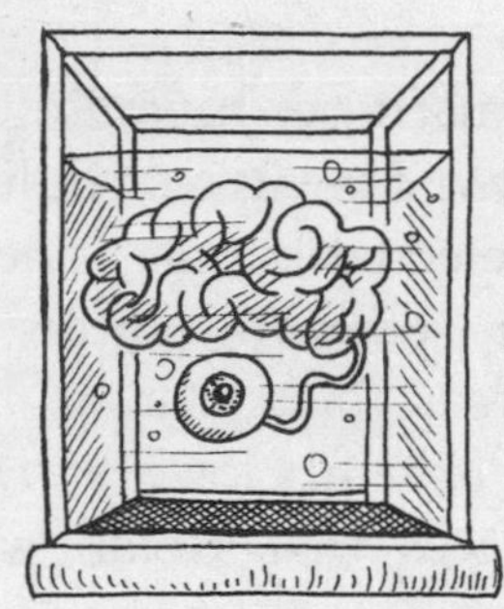

'William and Mary' – is one of Roald's strangest tales. It stars a man who has died before the story even starts! Before William died he agreed to have his brain removed and kept alive, floating in a glass tank! His brain is still conscious and can still think. He even has one eye left attached to it so he can still see. The experiment is a success. Soon Mary, his wife, comes to visit him. Like all Roald's classic tales, there is a nasty twist in the end. . .

'Royal Jelly' tells what happens when a beekeeper obsessed with bees and their life-cycle begins to feed royal jelly from his beehive to his young baby. (Told you the stories were weird.)

'The Champion of the World' tells the tale of two poachers Claud and Gordon. Together they decide to set an all time world record for poaching (i.e. nicking) pheasants from a local wood using a combination of raisins and sleeping pills. Sound familiar? It will to anyone who's ever read *Danny the Champion of the World.* Roald was never above recycling an idea, and used exactly the same plot a second time years later, retelling the tale for a younger audience and placing Danny and his dad at the heart of the action.

More success

When *Kiss Kiss* appeared it was another rather smashing success for Roald. Some of the American reviewers thought the new stories weren't up to the high standard of *Someone Like You*, but most critics gave the book a nod of approval. One reviewer even went as far as to say he thought Roald's new stories were rather like fairy stories for adults. (That reviewer should get a pretty good review himself, given what was about to happen to Roald's writing.)

The book sold well in America and in Britain. Roald's publisher in Britain had been so keen to publish it he even agreed to give Roald a royalty of 12.5% instead of the usual 10%! (A royalty means that the writer gets a share, or percentage, of the price of every book sold. So the better a book sells, the more money the author makes.) And once again, it didn't just appear in the

USA and the UK. Publishers from around the world translated the stories into their own languages to publish in their own countries. The money from all those sales would take a good few years to filter through to Roald. When it did though, he finally began to earn BIG time. In a way the success of *Kiss Kiss* gave Roald a huge problem. Or, more accurately, it made a problem that Roald already had seem even worse. It was a pretty big problem for someone who earns their living as a writer. Roald had completely run out of ideas for stories! But strangely enough, it was about to be the best thing that ever happened to him.

A PEACH OF AN IDEA

Roald's writing career was about to take a whole new direction. Although Roald was right out of fresh ideas for his short stories, he was still desperate to write.

ROALD'S SECRET WRITING DIARY
SUMMER 1960

Aggggggg! Disaster! Kiss Kiss is as big a success as my first book. Not much of a disaster, you might think, but it is when you're the author and you're completely out of ideas! I know dear old Alfred Knopf at the publishers will be on the phone soon asking for more stories for yet another book! I can't possibly tell him I've run out of stories. What would he say?! Every story seems

PETER & THE GIANT PINEAPPLE?

SALLY & THE GIANT STRAWBERRY?

GRAHAM AND THE GIANT GOOSEBERRY?

to be more difficult to write than the last. (And the last one was bally hard!)

Perhaps there is hope though. Last night I was putting the girls, Olivia and Tessa to bed when I had a marvellous idea. (Well, might be marvellous — might be something which will end my career!) Over the last few weeks, I've been telling them a bedtime story I've been making up to get them off to sleep. I wonder if this might make a rather smashing children's book?

QUENTIN AND THE GIANT KUMQUAT?

BETTY AND THE GIANT BANANA?

P.S. Note to self - of course, am rather worried I am wasting my time. I know Alfred wants more adult stories that will be taken seriously by important reviewers and the newspapers. Can easily imagine him throwing manuscript across room in the style of someone discarding unwanted piece of rubbish. I think it's a good story though, and so do my girls! Maybe worth the risk?

GORDON AND THE GIANT GRAPEFRUIT?

Roald went back to his writing shed and set to work. He sent the story, now called *James and the Giant Peach*, to his powerful publisher, then waited to hear what he thought about it. So what did Alfred Knopf think? Well, being a bit of a clever and wise man he didn't think anything. Alfred realized that he knew little about children's stories and so he passed Roald's manuscript on to someone who did – his children's editor, Virginie Fowler. So what did *she* reckon? She loved it. The next year, James and his bunch of weirdo friends made their debut in bookshops all over America.

The story begins with a poor orphan called James, who is sent to live with his two nasty aunts called Aunt Sponge and Aunt Spiker. They treat him like a slave, but things soon change when a strange old man gives James a bag full of magic. James accidentally drops the bag in the garden and suddenly the old barren tree there grows an amazing and fantastic giant peach. It's the size of a house! Inside the moist and beautiful peach, James finds a whole gang of new friends – strange talking insects that have grown as big as humans! Soon the peach gets so heavy it rolls from the tree and goes tumbling across the English countryside. It crashes right over a tall cliff and plummets into the ocean! And that's just the start of James' adventures!

Roald's idea for the plot of *James* was very different from the kind of plots he'd been writing in his short stories for adults. As he sat in his daughters' bedroom in the evenings, what on earth inspired him to think up such a strange story? A story about...

1 Someone who is unappreciated at home.

2 Someone who is given a surprise gift by a mysterious stranger.

3 Someone who meets lots of colourful new friends who help him escape his boring life.

4 Someone who goes on a voyage to America by sea.

5 Someone who escapes by taking flight.

6 Someone who arrives in the Big Apple and makes a bit of a splash.

7 Someone who becomes famous and writes a book.

Looking at James' adventures like that, maybe it's not too hard to see what could have inspired Roald after all.

James and the Giant Peach came out in America in 1961. (It wasn't published in Britain till ages later – much to Roald's annoyance.) Some reviewers loved the book. One critic even thought that it was as good as *Alice in Wonderland*. Others didn't like Roald's writing style and warned their readers not to buy it. The warning didn't work, though. Adult critics might not all like Roald's storytelling, but the audience he was writing for loved it. The book began to sell.

New tales

Back at home, Roald had already started telling his daughters a new bedtime story. In his special 'Ideas Notebook' he had jotted down that a chocolate factory might be a good place to set a story. *Charlie and the Chocolate Factory* took him nine months of full-time work to turn it from a bedtime story into a novel. Roald worked just as hard and re-wrote just as much for his children's books as he had for his adult short stories. That's one reason why they're so good. His description of Mr Wonka's magical factory is Roald's writing at its best:

WILLY WONKA'S CHOCOLATE FACTORY
GREAT IRON ENTRANCE GATES
WIDE MAIN CORRIDOR WITH PINKS WALLS
THE CHOCOLATE ROOM
OOMPA-LOOMPA VILLAGE
GLASS LIFT – can go anywhere in building.
THE OOMPA-LOOMPAS
VIKING STYLE BOAT – made from hollowed-out giant boiled sweet

THE TESTING ROOM
THE INVENTING ROOM
THE NUT ROOM
MOUNTAIN OF FUDGE
OIL WELL GUSHERS but with chocolate instead of oil.
LAKE OF THICK CARAMEL
ROCK CANDY DEPOSITS
MINUSLAND inhabited by...
GROOLIES

Roald the perfectionist

The first title Roald had for the book was 'Charlie's Chocolate Boy'. The story went through many different drafts as the perfectionist Roald rewrote it. Here are just a few of the changes Roald made to the story as he worked on it:

- The famous Oompa-Loompas who run the factory and do all the hard work spent the first draft of the story being called the Whipple-Scrumpets – before they got their proper name.
- In the early versions, there were seven golden tickets up for grabs not just five! Seven seemed to be too many, though, and slowed down the action. One child that Roald cut from the story was called Marvin Prune – a boy who was full of conceit. The other was a girl whose parents let her do exactly what she liked. She went by the wonderful name of Miranda Mary Piker.

- Roald also cut a whole chapter from the book. It was all about some white crystals called 'Spotty Powder'. You ate some at breakfast and the big red spots it gave you were guaranteed to get you off school for the day. Charlie realizes Spotty Powder would be particularly useful if you were expecting an exam. The Spotty Powder also accounted for the repulsive Miranda Mary Piker's exit from the book. She and her father disappeared while trying to stop the tricky powder being made.

- The story had a different ending as well. In Roald's earlier version, Charlie opened a huge chocolate shop in the centre of the city. The shop was just as grand as Willy Wonka's factory. It was nine floors high, staffed by exactly 100 assistants, and sold life-size chocolate elephants!

Of course there were some disagreements between Roald and his editor, Virginie Fowler – the same editor who'd worked on *James*. Ms Fowler thought it was a mistake to put any jokes for adults in the book. Roald, on the other hand, wanted to please both audiences. He knew if parents were reading the book aloud to their children then they'd probably be very grateful for a few jokes aimed at them. Ms Fowler didn't like some of his references to smelly rubbish and rotting food either. As usual, Roald won most of the arguments. He probably thought he had been proved right too. (He usually did.)

When it came out, *Charlie and the Chocolate Factory* was an even bigger success than *James*. It was published in America in September 1964 and sold over 10,000 in its first month, compared with sales of 6,000 for *James* in a whole year! Copies of *Charlie* were flying off the shelves quicker than you could say 'Willy Wonka'. *Charlie and the Chocolate Factory* still sells an amazing 100,000 copies every year!

After *Charlie* came out, Roald wrote an article for the *New York Times*. He made sure his readers knew just how long it had taken him to write his book and how hard he had worked on it. He also complained that it was difficult to make much money writing for children. This was one time when Roald would be proved completely wrong! By 1968, *Charlie* had sold over 600,000 copies in the USA! That's an awful lot of books and an awful lot of money for its author.

Rejected

It seems strange now, but although *Charlie* was a success in America, Roald had a great deal of trouble finding a publisher who liked it in Britain. Roald was annoyed and angry when several publishers turned both *James* and *Charlie* down on the grounds that they were too rude or too frightening for British children!

Roald felt that he should be shown more respect by companies in his own country. Anyway, the publishers that turned him down soon came to regret it. When the stories did appear in Britain, they sold masses.

A bit of bother

There was one part of *Charlie and the Chocolate Factory* that got Roald into heaps of trouble. It was his description of the Oompa-Loompas who do all the work in the factory. If you read the book today, you'll find that the strange little people are described as having golden hair and rose-white skin – a race of dwarf hippies. They didn't start out that way though. In the original book published in 1964, the Oompa-Loompas were described as being a tribe of black pygmies that Mr Wonka had shipped over from the darkest parts of Africa to work for him. Just slightly different, then!

When the book was first printed, no one at his publishers saw anything particularly wrong with having a tribe of black people slaving away in the depths of Willy Wonka's factory. Was it racist of Roald to portray them that way? Probably. But, you have to bear in mind a few other things as well. Firstly, Roald saw the book as a wild fantasy – he hadn't expected any of it to be taken seriously. Secondly, and most importantly, it was written several decades ago, when attitudes to different races and cultures were not the same as they are today. Roald recognized that himself, when the book was reprinted in a new edition in 1972. He rewrote several sections of the book, changing the old style Oompa-Loompas to the more modern fantasy hippie version that's in the book now.

A HAT TRICK OF HORRORS

If you have a box of tissues in the house, then you might want to get them for this next bit. During the 1960s Roald's little family was hit by three terrible disasters. We're not talking about things like going to the supermarket without your shopping list, or letting the bath overflow, either. We're talking real disasters – death, doom, and er . . . general unpleasantness. In some ways this period was the hardest and most difficult of Roald's entire life. The first horror involved a New York taxicab and Roald's four-month-old son, Theo. Before it was over, Roald had become an inventor.

Disaster number one: Theo

5th December 1960 was the Dahls' first date with disaster. The children's nanny was bringing them back from school for lunch. As she crossed a road, a taxi cab tried to jump the traffic light. The cab hit Theo's pram and sent it flying forwards into the side of a bus! As a result, Theo's skull was broken in several places. Doctors told the waiting Mr and Mrs Dahl that they expected

Theo to die. He didn't though. Instead, baby Theo was left with a condition called hydrocephalus, or water-on-the-brain. This meant there was fluid in Theo's little head that needed draining away.

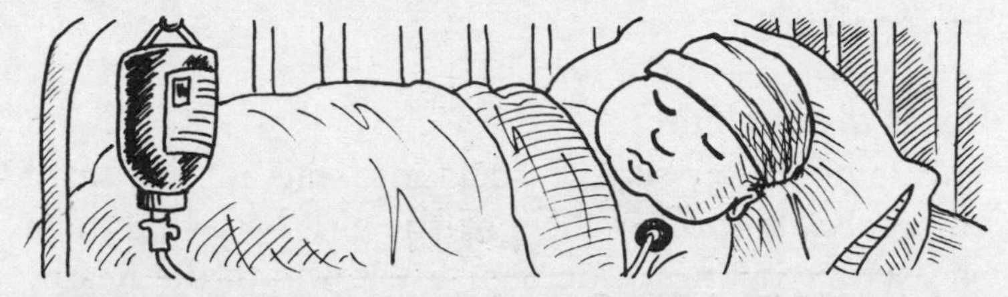

The best thing the hospital had (or ANY hospital had) was a valve and tube arrangement that released the fluid. The big problem was the valve kept getting clogged up. When it did, things became very uncomfortable for poor little Theo – because his head would literally swell and bulge with the extra fluid inside it! Ouch! The swelling would make him go blind and gave him a terrible fever. Seeing the terrible state his son was in, Roald began searching for a better solution. To his surprise he discovered there were thousands of children around the world in the same unhappy position as Theo.

Now we're coming up to a typical moment of pure Roald. Most other people would probably have mumbled something about doctors being useless and quietly shuffled off home to be depressed. Not Roald. Roald decided there had to be a better answer and that HE was going to find it.

The first thing Roald did was to move the entire family. He wanted to get away from the busy streets of New York back to the quiet of the English countryside and the safety of Gipsy House. Maybe he could find an answer there?

Roald the inventor

The family soon settled back into life in the small village. Roald tried to cheer up the girls by taking them on exciting outings. One regular trip was to the nearby hills to fly model gliders. The girls loved watching the models in flight and Roald could imagine himself as a dashing pilot once more. During the glider trips, Roald became friends with Stanley Wade, an engineer who made tiny engines for model aircraft as a hobby.

Roald was still grappling with Theo's problem. One day Kenneth Till, a neuro-surgeon, explained to Roald exactly what happened when the valve in Theo's head got blocked. Roald had a sudden thought.

If anyone could build a better valve, it was his aircraft-flying friend. He was an engineer. He was used to solving problems. And he was used to working small! Stanley Wade designed a new and much better valve in less than a month. The three men worked on developing it together. It would be called the Wade-Dahl-Till valve and the three men all agreed they would accept no profits from their invention.

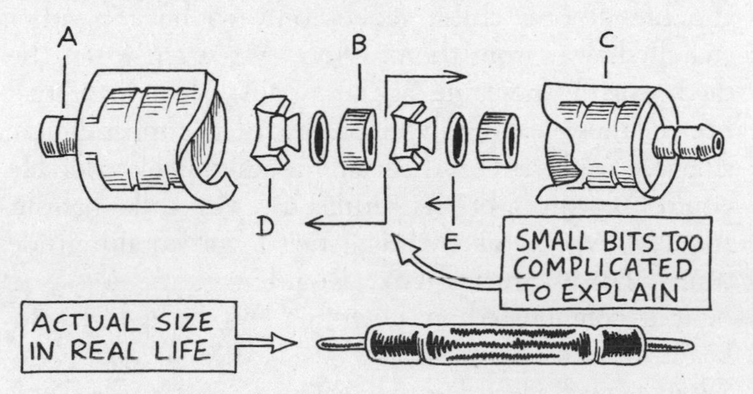

The valve worked much better than the old one and was used to help treat over 3,000 other children who had the same problem. Ironically, the new valve was never used on Theo. He suddenly began to get better anyway. Roald's determination to help his own son, though, had saved many lives around the world. Theo went on to live a full and happy life and for many years remained living near Gipsy House.

Disaster number two: Olivia

With Theo on the mend, and the family safe in England, Roald's life seemed to be back on track. Sadly it didn't last. Disaster was about to strike again, and this time there would be no happy ending. Following an outbreak of measles at her school, Olivia (Roald and Pat's oldest daughter) caught the illness. Measles isn't usually dangerous, but her condition became worse and worse and she suddenly slipped into a coma. An ambulance rushed her to hospital, but it was too late. She died the same night.

Roald and Pat had spent the last two years fighting for the life of one child, Theo, only to have another snatched away from them. Olivia was seven when she died, exactly the same age as Roald's older sister had been all those years ago when she had died of appendicitis. Olivia's death hit him as hard as anything could. He could hardly bring himself to talk about it and most of his feelings stayed bottled up inside him. After she died, Roald built a complicated and very beautiful rock garden by Olivia's grave. He collected rare miniature plants from all over the world and carefully moved them into position. Creating the rock garden took him a solid month of work. Afterwards, Pat thought that it had helped him in some small way.

Roald found that writing was impossible for many months after Olivia died. Sometimes he wondered if he would ever be able to write again. Meanwhile Pat took the first acting job that she was offered. The family needed the money and she hoped that working might help her cope with her grief. Whenever Roald went into his writing shed, though, things were just as difficult as ever. As he sat facing the blank pages waiting for him, his thoughts always turned to the same thing. . .

Disaster number three: Pat

You might think that after those two tragedies the Dahls deserved some peace. Not a bit of it. While the family were in Hollywood Pat suffered a terrible stroke. It was so bad one newspaper reported that she had actually died!

The Hollywood Times

FILM ACTRESS PATRICIA NEAL DIES AT 39!

In fact, she hadn't. Here's what really happened.

The Dahly Telegraph

17 February 1965

PATRICIA NEAL RUSHED TO HOSPITAL AFTER STROKE!

Oscar-winning actress, Patricia Neal, was rushed to hospital last night after she had a massive stroke. On reaching the UCLA Medical Centre she underwent many hours of brain surgery in an effort to save her life.

The blonde blue-eyed actress was at her Hollywood home when the stroke happened. She was giving her children a bedtime bath when suddenly the beautiful star felt a sharp pain in her head and her vision became blurry. Luckily, her husband – the English writer, Roald Dahl – took decisive action. He immediately rang for an ambulance and arranged for top brain surgeon Charles Carton to meet them at the hospital.

When Miss Neal arrived he discovered that an artery in her head had burst, sending a jet of blood into her brain. The operation to save Miss Neal lasted over seven hours and involved a trapdoor being cut into the left side of her head with a saw! Miss Neal survived the operation but was left barely able to speak and unable to move her right side. Hollywood wishes her a speedy recovery.

Pat's progress

It was going to take a lot more than good wishes for Pat to make a full recovery, though. The doctors told Roald the next three months were vital. If Pat didn't make good progress in that time, then she might never recover. Roald did what he had done when Theo was injured – as soon as possible he moved the whole family back to the safety of Gipsy House. This time he brought along a nurse or two as well, just for good measure. Roald decided Pat needed therapy – and lots of it. His plan was to bully her back to health. He organized a rota of people so she would have six hours of lessons and therapy every single day. Some people thought Roald was pushing his sick wife too hard and making her work too much. Others thought that what he was doing might be her best hope to get better. Often Pat herself would be depressed and fed up and sometimes she called her husband Roald the Rotten because of his slave-driving ways. Slowly, however, over long months, she started to improve.

The nosey newspapers were interested in how she was doing as well. Her stroke and her recovery were the subject of many articles and even a book. Writer Barry Farrell went to stay with the Dahls and rather fell under Roald's spell. He wrote a book called *Pat and Roald* which told the story of Pat's medical mishaps and was rather flattering to our hero Roald in the process.

After Pat's recovery many people wrote to the Dahls at Gipsy House asking for advice with similar problems. So many that Roald wrote a special letter that could be copied and sent out detailing Pat's therapy. Hundreds of people asked for a copy. A couple of years after the stroke, Pat was even able to return to acting!

Babblements

Patricia had a habit of getting her words all twisted after she had had her stroke. She couldn't say the proper words for things and often said nonsense instead. A cigarette became an 'obligon' in her new language and she'd make serious announcements like 'If I don't have dinner soon I'll jake my dioddles!'

Roald remembered Pat's difficulties when he was writing his book, *The BFG* (which we'll hear more about on page 183). The thing most people remember about the Big Friendly Giant is his unusual way of speaking. Sometimes when you're reading the book, you almost need a translator, so here are some of the BFG's favourite most delumptious babblements twistlated into English (or thereabouts).

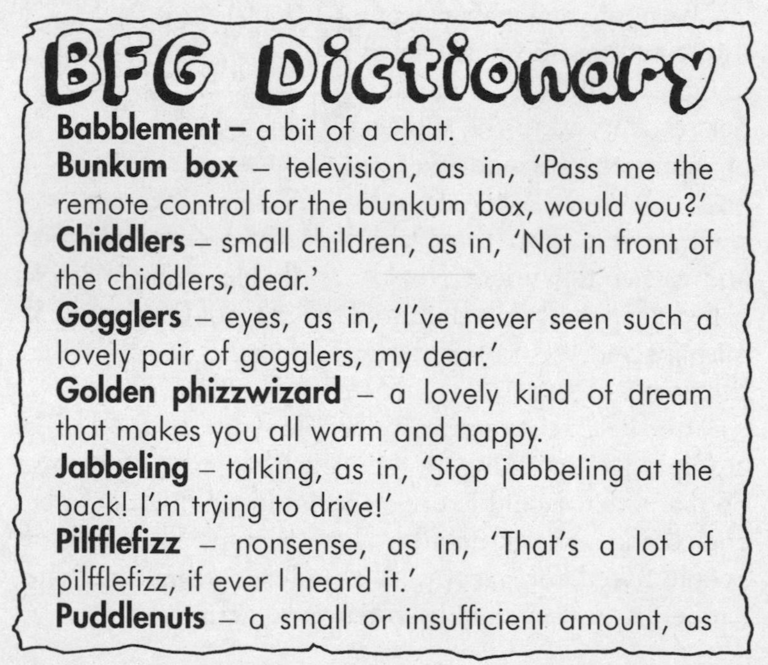

BFG Dictionary

Babblement – a bit of a chat.

Bunkum box – television, as in, 'Pass me the remote control for the bunkum box, would you?'

Chiddlers – small children, as in, 'Not in front of the chiddlers, dear.'

Gogglers – eyes, as in, 'I've never seen such a lovely pair of gogglers, my dear.'

Golden phizzwizard – a lovely kind of dream that makes you all warm and happy.

Jabbeling – talking, as in, 'Stop jabbeling at the back! I'm trying to drive!'

Pilfflefizz – nonsense, as in, 'That's a lot of pilfflefizz, if ever I heard it.'

Puddlenuts – a small or insufficient amount, as

in, 'Waiter, this serving of ice-cream is puddlenuts.'
Scrumdiddlyumptious – rather tasty.
Snozzcumbers – a giant vegetable covered in black and white stripes.
Swizzfiggling – lying, or pulling someone's leg, as in, 'Just who are you trying to swizzfiggle?'
Trogglehumper – a nasty nightmare that makes you wake up screaming.
Uckyslush – having an unpleasant flavour.
Whizzpopper – to break wind, as in 'Blimey! Who let off that terrible whizzpopper? 'This is only a small lift and now we will surely suffocate to death in moments.'

When it came out, *The BFG* proved to be a huge hit with readers all over the world.

Roald the screenwriter

During the 1960s Roald began to write something other than books. He started to write films. With all the accidents and illnesses befalling his poor family, there were some huge medical bills to pay! Roald wasn't able to work for six solid months after the death of Olivia, and when Pat had her stroke, she couldn't work either. Roald needed to earn serious money. Although film people had a reputation for sometimes treating writers quite badly, one thing was certainly true: Hollywood paid BIG BUCKS. Some of Roald's film scripts worked out very well, others sank without trace. Here are Roald's film projects from that time.

Title: *Oh Death, Where is Thy Sting-a-ling-a-ling*
What Roald did: Was asked to write the original screenplay with director Robert Altman.
What happened? Nothing. It all fell apart after an argument about money. With a title like that, maybe it was just as well!

Title: *36 Hours*
What Roald did: Sold MGM the rights to his story called 'Beware of the Dog.' They paid him $30,000 (about a quarter of a million dollars today). All Roald had to do was cash the cheque, thank you very much, and watch other people do all the hard work.
What happened? Big smiles all round Gipsy House.

Double-O-Dahl

Just when Roald needed money the most (after Pat's stroke) he was asked to write the biggest film project he was ever involved in. The name of the central hero was Bond, James Bond. Roald was asked to provide the screenplay for *You Only Live Twice*, the next Bond picture. The film was to star top heart-throb Sean Connery and be set in mysterious Japan. Before he started work, Roald made all sorts of noises pretending that such film work was beneath a writer of his immense talent.

Humbug. Bond would turn out to be the high point of Roald's ventures into screenwriting. For someone with Roald's imagination and sense of the fantastic, being asked to write a Bond script must have felt like being a kid let loose in a sweetshop. Helicopters, hidden secret bases, gorgeous girls and even spaceships.

The film took its title from another of Ian Fleming's Bond books, but the producers decided to drop the book's plot completely and make up their own. Space was very big in 1966. The Americans were racing to be the first to land on the moon. What better idea, then, than to have fiendish baddie Blofeld try and start Third World War by nicking American and Russian spaceships?

Most of the story was decided before Roald had even been given the job. For once, though, James Bond wasn't the star of the show. No, the real star was designer Ken Adams' amazing set for the evil SPECTRA's secret base. And where was the best place cunningly to conceal your secret base? Why, under a fake sliding lake in the hollowed out remains of a Japanese volcano, of course. Doh!

HERO'S ARMY (ARRIVING JUST IN NICK OF TIME)
FAKE LAKE (SORRY, NO FISHING - IT'S JUST PRETEND WATER)
HELICOPTER (HANDY FOR SHOPPING)
SECRET ROCKET FOR NICKING OTHER PEOPLE'S ROCKETS
MOVABLE HELIPORT
CONTROL ROOM (GREAT PLACE TO START NEXT WORLD WAR)
VILLAIN'S ARMY (NOT A GOOD CHOICE OF JOB IF HOPING FOR A LONG CAREER)
NOT SO FAST! etc...
SIGH
VILLAIN - ERNST STAVRO BLOFELD (BOO! HISS!)
CURSES! etc...
HERO - 007 (HOORAY!)
HERO'S EXOTIC JAPANESE BIRD (OO-ER!)
VILLAIN'S WHITE CAT (BLESS)

Roald wrote most of the script for the film at Gipsy House. A large chauffeur-driven Rolls Royce would sometimes call at the gate to collect his latest draft! Roald also joined the cast and crew when they flew to Japan for filming. When it came out, in 1967, *You Only Live Twice* was a hit all over the world. It cost $10 million to make and at the box-office it took over ten times that.

Title: *Chitty Chitty Bang Bang*

What Roald did: He was commissioned to write the screenplay from Ian Fleming's children's book *Chitty Chitty Bang Bang*. Five weeks before it was supposed to begin shooting Roald had only written one third of the film! Even worse, the producer and director hated what little he had written.
What happened? The director, Ken Hughes, ended up writing his own script in a rush just before the cameras rolled. Roald got paid huge amounts of money for doing nothing and his name stayed on the film's credits.

Title: *The Night Digger*
What Roald did: He bought the rights to turn a new novel by Joy Cowley called *Nest in a Falling Tree* into a

film. Roald wrote the screenplay and Pat took the leading role, playing a woman who is recovering from a stroke. Sounds like a perfect combination? Well, no it wasn't.

What happened? Both Roald and Pat signed a deal in which they only got paid when the film made a profit. When it came out, it got terrible reviews – 'an artfully photographed mess' said the *Hollywood Reporter*. No one went to see it and they didn't make a bean.

Roald's next film was a project that was very close to his heart. In fact, it was adapted from a book by his favourite author in the entire world – himself. Roald had been asked to write the film script for his own *Charlie and the Chocolate Factory*.

The first thing the film people did was to change the title – it was soon *Willy Wonka and the Chocolate Factory*. Roald flew to LA and stayed in the Beverly Hills Hotel while he wrote the screenplay. Sounds rather smashing – except that it wasn't. Roald was furious when he found out the film's director had hired someone else to rewrite his script.

The second version had a lot of new dialogue, a few new adventures in the factory, and a different ending. Roald didn't like the changes, but there was nothing he could do. In Hollywood, it's not writers who really matter. *Willy Wonka* was the last film Roald wrote.

Screenplays like the one for James Bond had seen Roald survive the hard times and high medical bills of the last few years. His first two children's books were selling fantastically well in America. Together they had sold nearly a million copies, earning Roald buckets of cash. Suddenly, he didn't need any more well-paid film jobs. Roald decided it was time to go back to his shed and write more children's books.

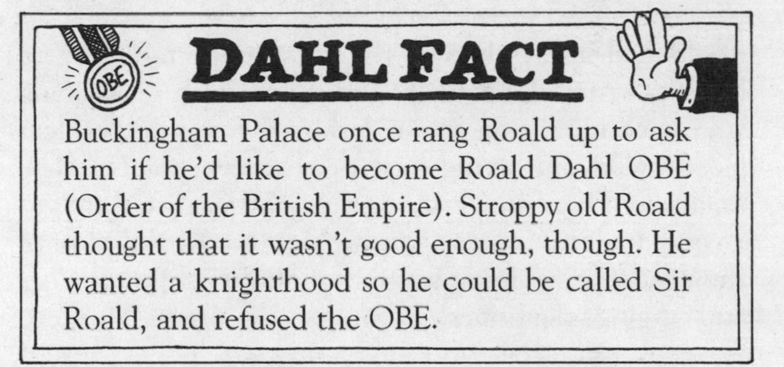

Buckingham Palace once rang Roald up to ask him if he'd like to become Roald Dahl OBE (Order of the British Empire). Stroppy old Roald thought that it wasn't good enough, though. He wanted a knighthood so he could be called Sir Roald, and refused the OBE.

WARNING: WRITER AT WORK

Roald had always known the most important part of being a writer was actually getting on with it. Keeping your backside sitting at the desk is the biggest problem faced by anyone trying to write, however famous they might be. There are always so many other nice things to go and do. It was especially a problem for Roald. Most of the time, Gipsy House was full of adults, children, dogs and ringing telephones!

Soon after they had moved in, Roald realized that if he was going to get any work done he needed a secret hideaway. Somewhere he could go to write and be certain of being left alone. He didn't need to look far for the answer.

The writing shed

In the garden was a large shed. It was hidden behind the greenhouse and well away from the house. It would be perfect. The paint was peeling off the walls inside and the floor was a mess, but Roald didn't care about mere details like that. A bit of squalor never hurt anyone. Roald set about transforming the gloomy shed into a writing den. He moved in a filing cabinet so he had somewhere to store papers and other things. He added a couple of electric lamps for better light, and a heater for the winter. He ran a wire from a light in the shed back to the house. Pat used it to signal him. One flash meant he was needed at the house to say hello to a visitor or that food was ready. A signal of two quick flashes meant an emergency of some kind and he should leg it back at top speed!

To get real peace and quiet, Roald had to fight off wild animals. Well, squirrels and cows. The squirrels scampered around outside the hut and often distracted Roald when he was writing. Work was all that mattered when Roald was inside the shed, so he put a plastic curtain across the window to block out the rascally rodents. Often there were several cows wandering around the grounds of Gipsy House. If Roald ever forgot to shut the windows, he'd come back to the shed to find one eating his newly installed curtains!

Another essential thing for the writing shed was a huge wastepaper bin. Roald usually corrected mistakes and rewrote stories as he went along. We've seen how hard he worked to get his stories just right. For example, his picture book *The Enormous Crocodile* went through many different versions before he finally found one he liked. That story was only 35 pages long, but Re-writing Roald got through 314 pages writing it! That's a lot of waste paper!

During the shed's many years of use, Roald developed the perfect system to make sure he could write in comfort. He needed to as well. A lot of his books were written when he was quite old, and he had to look after himself. The first thing he did was pick the most comfortable old armchair he could find as his writing chair. He added a sleeping bag which he pulled up to his waist to keep himself warm when it was cold. A suitcase on the floor in front of the armchair acted as a comfy foot rest to keep him at just the right angle. When Roald was sitting down, he put a green board made of wood across the arms of the chair, giving him a nice steady surface to work on.

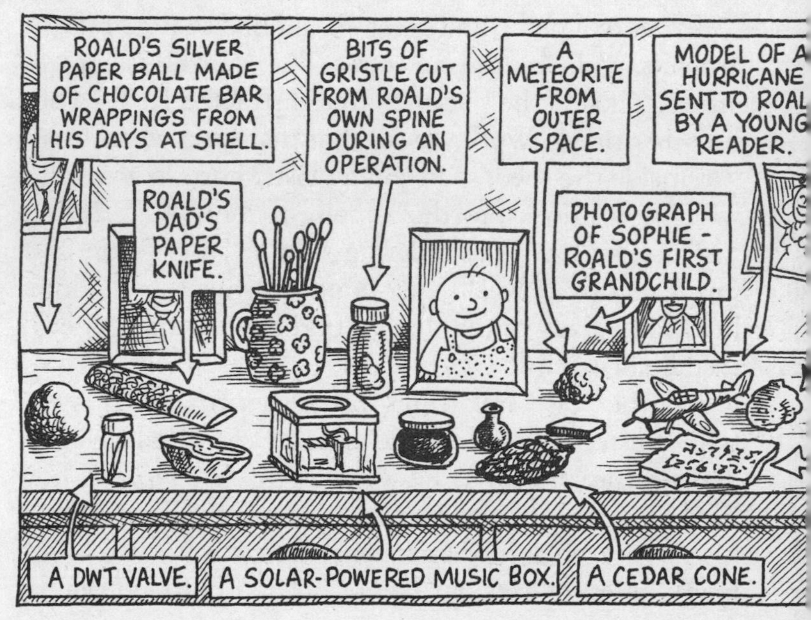

Next to Roald's writing chair was a table covered with weird bits and bobs he had saved over the years. (Roald's collecting urge again.) Just like Roald, some of them are funny, some sentimental, and some just gruesome.

Writing routine

Like most writers, Roald had a regular routine he tried to stick to as much as possible. He would usually slink off to his quiet hut at about ten in the morning. He worked until 12:30 when he would go back to the house for some lunch. When he was older, he'd often have a rest in the afternoon, before returning to the writing shed for another session between four and six.

Writers are often a superstitious bunch when it comes to how they work. Roald had to have exactly the right materials. They included a pad of yellow American

Legal paper (always yellow – it had to be yellow). And most importantly, a particular brand of pencil, and there had to be six of them. Not five. And not seven. It always had to be six. Roald wrote his books longhand – without using a typewriter or computer. Using pencils let him rub out and correct mistakes as he went along. The only other thing he had to have was an automatic pencil sharpener to keep them ready for action. Roald once wrote to his publisher in America complaining he could no longer find the right sort of pencil in England. They sent someone out of the office to track some down for him. Talk about fussy!

Hard work

Roald often told people writing was more to do with perspiration than inspiration. He didn't think up his stories in one sudden blinding flash of genius. He usually started with a small seed of an idea and worked very hard to turn it into a full length book.

One of Roald's favourite stories about writing was to do with a famous Russian composer called Stravinsky. People were always asking this great genius where he got his brilliant ideas from? (Probably because they hoped to copy him and do the same.) They expected him to say something like he got his ideas while out walking through the beautiful Russian woods at midnight. Or perhaps watching a sunset over snow-capped mountains.

But Stravinsky always answered the question by telling people the unglamorous truth. He got his ideas for music sitting at his piano, working.

Roald was the same. He had no secret shortcuts to writing a great story. No hidden tricks. He used his imagination and his talent, but most of all he worked hard. Every single sentence in all of his stories was carefully crafted until it said exactly what he wanted it to say.

Back to books

In the 1960s, Roald spent much of his time on film work and recovering from the three great disasters that had hit his family. In that time, though, he did manage two shorter books.

The Magic Finger, published in 1966, tells the story of a girl who gets angry and puts the 'magic finger' on the Greg family who live next door. The girl doesn't like the father and his sons shooting animals and birds. First the magic finger affects their aim, then they wake up the next morning to find the whole family have shrunk to the size of birds and have grown wings! A family of real ducks move into the Gregg's house forcing the family to build a bird's nest in a nearby tree. Things get even worse for the Greggs when the ducks soon begin hunting them with guns! *The Magic Finger* is a simple but charming tale that takes the ducks' side against the hunters and asks the question, how would you like your family to be shot at for fun?

Roald's next book was *Fantastic Mr. Fox*, which he originally just called 'The Fox'. Everyone at his publishers was pleased when they got a new story from their best-selling author. There was only one problem. No one liked it. The story started with three mean farmers laying siege to the Foxes' home – just like in the final book – but then they were rather different:

Roald's publishers weren't too keen on telling people it was OK to steal from shops. And anyway, Mr. Fox's one-stop shop seemed to be too easy an answer to the Fox family's troubles. Roald's editor decided Mr. Fox should have to make a bit more effort before he got what he wanted. He sent Roald a list of suggestions for improving the story. Just for once, Roald didn't get all rude. In fact, he liked his editor's ideas so much that Roald put them all into the story. Here's how the second version went:

In the new version Mr. Fox had to put a lot more work into becoming a hero. AND he was stealing from the evil old farmers not an innocent supermarket! The book came out in 1970.

Charlie in space

For Roald's next full-length work he went back to some old friends. Roald decided there was another story to be told about Charlie and that mad chocolate-making genius, Mr Willy Wonka. As we've seen, Roald was never afraid of re-using an idea. The opening of the new book put Mr Wonka and the Bucket family in orbit high above the earth with an American space capsule. Sounds just a bit like the space scenes in *You Only Live Twice*, doesn't it?

ROALD'S BRILLIANT BOOKSHELF

CHARLIE AND THE GREAT GLASS ELEVATOR

Charlie and the Great Glass Elevator carries on immediately from the end of Charlie and the Chocolate Factory. The magical lift containing Mr Wonka, Charlie, and his whole family, is accidentally sent into orbit around the earth! They spot an American space capsule and then America's giant Space Hotel. Mr Wonka docks the lift at the hotel and they soon discover that the place has been invaded by deadly space aliens called Vermicious Knids!

The jelly-like Knids attack Charlie and his friends and they flee. Pretty soon it's up to Mr Wonka and Charlie to save the American spaceship from the terrible people-eating aliens! The second part of the adventure sees the lift returning to Earth. Mr Wonka then persuades Charlie's old grandparents to take some Wonka-Vite pills to make them young again, but they get greedy and take too many! Grandma becomes trapped in a strange spooky place called Minusland. Charlie and Mr Wonka voyage deep into the Earth in a dangerous effort to save her!

Most people thought the book started well with the adventures in space and the attacking aliens, but that the second half was too full of bits and pieces for it to be among Roald's best books.

Roald in ruins

As Roald was getting older and older, his body was ever so slightly falling apart. He spent a fair amount of each day in pain either with his bad back or other bits. (No wonder he was so rude sometimes!) Here's just a few of the things that gave him trouble in his later years.

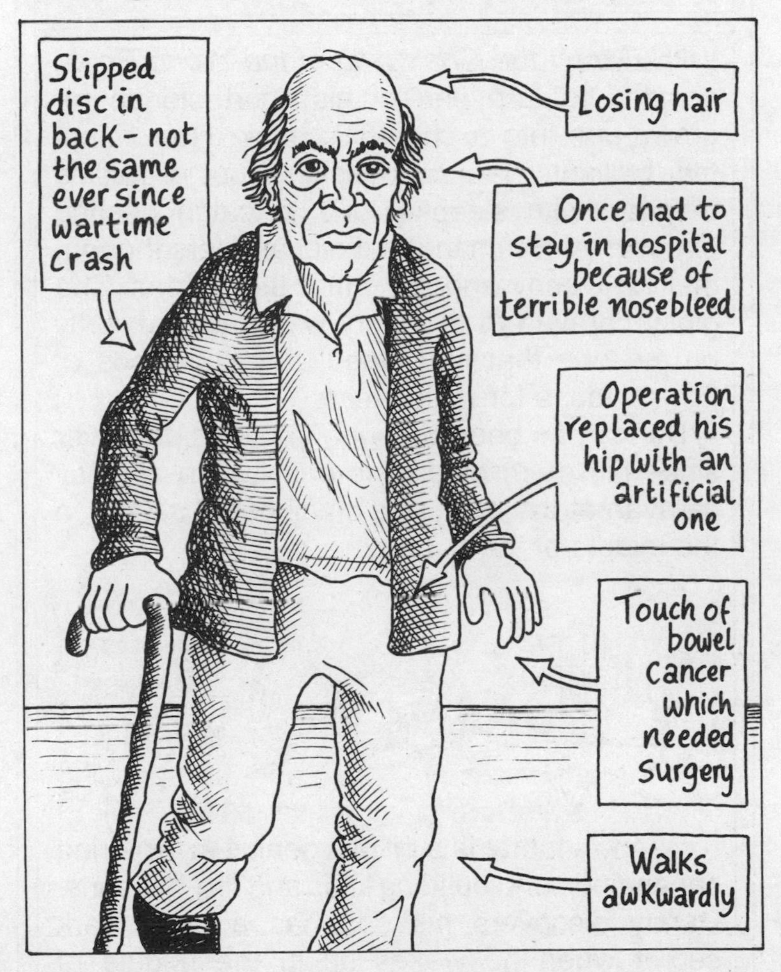

A champion book

With *Danny the Champion of the World* Roald decided to turn one of his short stories for grown-ups into a children's book. Roald kept the brilliant idea of poachers using raisins drugged with sleeping pills to catch nesting pheasants. He changed the characters though, making Danny and his father the heroes. The gipsy caravan in the story was based exactly on the one that had stood in the grounds of Gipsy House for many years.

Danny has been brought up by his dad ever since his mum died. The pair live in a gipsy caravan at the back of a small petrol station in the middle of the country.

Danny's father is a bit of a genius at repairing car engines and building kites and fire-balloons. Danny discovers his dad has a deep dark secret when he wakes up in the middle of the night and finds his father missing. When his dad returns he has to confess that he is a secret night-time poacher! Danny's dad lets him into a few poacher's secrets and soon they become what must be the best father and son poaching team in the world.

A few years after *Danny* came out, Roald tried his hand at writing another novel for adults. Roald's second novel was called *My Uncle Oswald*. The story was an attempt at comedy with Uncle Oswald involved in a strange plot in which he has to meet as many famous geniuses as he can. It was this book that Roald and his publishers both tried to say was his first adult novel – conveniently forgetting the failure of *Some Time Never* way back in 1949. But *Oswald* wasn't much more successful and got Roald very mixed reviews.

As Roald got older, he sometimes seemed to get even ruder! One night he went to the Curzon House Club to have dinner. Rude Roald decided he didn't like the way it had just been redecorated and started to complain about it. Then he started moaning about other people eating dinner there. The club threw him out and later ripped up his membership card so he couldn't ever go back!

Roald the TV Star

In 1979, Roald's short stories were turned into a television series called *Tales of the Unexpected.* Each episode was half an hour long and was introduced by Roald himself. Our boy was filmed sitting in a comfy armchair in front of a roaring fire in his home (actually a fake set in a TV studio). Roald got the chance to play his favourite role of wise old storyteller – this time to the entire country! (And then the rest of the world as the series was also sold to 70 other countries.)

The series ran for many years and started using stories by other writers after they had adapted the best 25 of Roald's own twisted tales. Weirdly, *Tales of the Unexpected* is probably best remembered for the woman in white who appeared every week during the opening credits performing a bizarre dance routine.

More brilliant books

Even though he was getting older, Roald was about to enjoy the most productive writing period in his entire life! Pretty soon he'd be dashing off books like they were going out of fashion. First, though, he needed to meet two very important people. One was a professional partner – the other was going to become his second wife. We'll do the professional partner first:

The Idiot's Ten Second Guide to . . . Quentin Blake

Many different artists had worked on Roald's books before, but none of them had quite hit it off with either the words or the author who wrote them. With Quentin it was different. His pictures were the perfect partners for Roald's words – and the two enjoyed working closely together. Just for once, Roald agreed with everyone else who thought they made a dream team, with Roald doing the writing and Quentin providing his wonderful pictures to illustrate Roald's words. In fact, Quentin became so associated with Roald he would go back and draw all of Roald's other books, like *Charlie* and *James*, as well!

Many of Roald and Quentin's early books together were quite short. Here's just a taster of what they were about:

George's Marvellous Medicine – a tale of revenge as George strikes back at his granny for being so very horrible to him. He cooks up a special medicine for her to take which has very unexpected results.

The Twits – another of Roald's many stories about revenge. (Maybe we should have called him Revengeful Roald?) Mr and Mrs Twit are a disgusting married couple always playing cruel tricks on one another. But they're not just cruel to each other: they save their most extreme nastiness for the birds and monkeys in their garden. When the visiting Roly-Poly Bird helps the monkeys escape, it's time for revenge!

Revolting Rhymes is a collection of comic verse that rewrites famous fairy stories like

Cinderella, Snow White, and Little Red Riding Hood. Roald added black humour, unexpected twists, and a good helping of violence to the well-known fairy tale plots.

Meanwhile, something even bigger was happening at Gipsy House. It really was in the newspapers at the time – here's how a report might have looked:

The Dahly Gossip

17 November 1983

THE DAHLS DIVORCE

Here's a real tale of the unexpected from Roald Dahl! He and Patricia Neal announced a divorce today! Looks like poor old Pat is going back to the USA while Dahl (67) stays at their family home with new love, Felicity 'Liccy' Crossland, 20 years his junior. Liccy was Patricia's friend, but when she was introduced to Roald, 'they took one look at each other and – wham! – Pat was out of the picture,' a reliable source squealed to us.

With his two new partners, Roald wrote more children's books in the next ten years than in the rest of his life put together! Throughout the 1980s Roald published a book nearly every year. . .

ROALD'S BRILLIANT BOOKSHELF

THE BFG

The BFG, or Big Friendly Giant, stomped into bookstores in 1982. The BFG is a 10-metre-tall giant who stalks through the night, delivering wonderful dreams into the heads of sleeping children. He lives in a cave where he has thousands and thousands of dreams – each carefully labelled and stored in a glass bottle.

The BFG was another invention of Roald's that started out as a bedtime tale for his children. For this one though, Roald more than just told the story. Sometimes he acted out the part as well! After he had told the girls the latest adventures of the BFG, Roald would creep outside, put a ladder under their window, then climb up and pretend to be the BFG himself!

The BFG first appeared in *Danny the Champion of the World* where Danny's dad tells him about the strange dream-catching giant. In the book, *The BFG*, the giant is spotted by Sophie, the heroine, one night when she can't get to sleep. He grabs her and carries her back to his cave in Giant Country. Sophie learns about the other giants – all horrible man-, woman-, and child-eating giants who run all over the world gobbling up 'human beans' whenever they get hungry.

The Witches

Roald's next book was *The Witches*, which we've already met on page 22. Like many of his stories, *The Witches* changed a lot as Roald wrote and rewrote it. Early versions of the book contained a lot of stories about Roald's own boyhood adventures in Norway. His editor, Stephen Roxburgh, suggested leaving them out of this book, saying that perhaps they might make another very different book in the near future. (They would!) Another thing his editor dared to suggest was changing the role of the greedy food-grabbing Bruno Jenkins. In Roald's first draft, it was Bruno who actually defeated the witches! Weird, eh? Again, Roald actually listened to the advice carefully and agreed with most of his editor's comments. He must have been glad that he did, because the next year *The Witches* did what no other Dahl children's book had done – it won a major award in Britain! Modest old Roald (yeah, right) was presented with the Whitbread Prize for 1983. (He gave the £3,000 prize money to a hospice for sick children.)

Not all Roald's books were as well received as *The Witches*. His collection of comic verse, *Dirty Beasts*, was criticized as being too frightening and likely to give its readers nightmares! One of the verses, for example, featured a large and clever pig who turns on his farmer owner and eats him! The trouble with *Dirty Beasts* was that, although they were well drawn, the illustrations by Rosemary Fawcett seemed to increase the horror of Roald's stories (which were pretty horrible to start with!). When the book was reprinted a few years later, it appeared with more gentle and humorous pictures by Roald's fave artist Quentin Blake.

Boy's own stories

Remember the stories about Roald's own childhood that his editor had suggested cutting from *The Witches*? Well, never one to waste material, Roald turned them into two volumes of autobiography. The first one, called *Boy* (published in 1984), tells the story of Roald's family from the time his father left Norway up until the moment when Roald was given his assignment in Africa by Shell. Roald continued the story in *Going Solo*, which came out in 1986, and covers Roald's adventures in the heat of Africa and all his daring wartime deeds (including a far more accurate retelling of his wartime plane crash).

think perhaps Roald might have been thinking of his own school days?)

Matilda Wormwood is the daughter of a dodgy used-car salesman and a mother addicted to bingo. She's supersmart and learned to read when she was just three years old. Matilda loves books while her dull parents prefer bad TV. After her father complains about her for the millionth time, she superglues his hat to his head and then tricks him into dying his hair bright silver for revenge.

Soon Matilda is sent to a school run by mad headmistress Miss Trunchbull. Miss Trunchbull has a frightening reputation for inventing new ways of torturing and punishing pupils who step out of line. Matilda's favourite teacher at the school is Miss Honey. She's the only person who really appreciates Matilda for being smart. Miss Honey's problem is that she's poorer than a church mouse because she has been cheated out of her rightful inheritance. When Matilda's super-powered brain begins to develop special powers she sees her chance to help Miss Honey. . .

Matilda is one of Roald's longest books and perfectly captures the spirit of children being treated unfairly and getting their own back on the awful adults who boss them around.

When *Matilda* came out in 1988 it became Roald's fastest-selling book in nearly 50 years of writing! It also won him the Children's Book Award for that year.

Last words

Matilda was the last full-length book that Roald would write. His four final works were all shorter stories for a slightly younger audience. The first of the four was *Rhyme Stew*, another collection of retellings of famous stories like 'Hansel and Gretel' and 'Aladdin'. His next book has one of the strangest titles of any of Roald's works, *Esio Trot*. The two words are in fact 'tortoise' spelt backwards. It's a fitting title because the book tells how the old and lonely Mr Hoppy sets out to win the love of Mrs Silver by the ingenious use of 140 tortoises.

The Minipins is a picture book about a boy, Billy, who escapes from the safe, protective world of his mother's house and enters the Forest of Sin. In the woods he is hunted by the terrible Spittler beast and discovers a race of small people, the Minipins, who are no taller than peas. The Minipins live in the trees and fly through the air on the backs of birds.

The last book that Roald ever wrote was created for charity. It was called *The Vicar of Nibbleswicke* and featured a young vicar, the Reverend Lee, who suddenly finds himself speaking certain words backwards. Roald signed over all the rights to the story to raise money for the Dyslexia Institute.

Lights, camera, Roald!

When an author's books sell as many copies as Roald's do then it's usually not long before film producers come knocking. If people loved Roald's stories as a book, it figures that they'd love them even more as a motion picture, right?

Roald had his own opinions of the film adaptations of his books (at least the ones he lived long enough to see). *The Witches* was made into a film at the very end of Roald's life and he wasn't at all happy, calling it "utterly appalling." He hated the fact that the filmmakers changed the ending of *The Witches* so that the boy became human again. Roald advised (in a very loud voice) as many readers as he could not to go and see it!

In 2005, top American director Tim Burton filmed a new adaptation of *Charlie and the Chocolate Factory*. One of Hollywood's biggest actors, Johnny Depp, took the central role of Willy Wonka. The musical adventure was a big chocolate-covered hit with both critics and audiences around the world and earned nearly $500 million! The part of Roald that liked making money from his writing would have loved that. *Charlie and the Chocolate Factory* has proved such a hit that it's also become a video game and a theme park ride.

Fantastic Mr Fox became a brilliant stop-motion animated film with Wes Anderson as the director. Wes Anderson is often described as "quirky", which means he's a bit mad but very talented. His version of *Fantastic Mr Fox* was a big hit too and was described as "a delightfully funny feast for the eyes."

Roald Dahl's *Esio Trot*, his romantic tale of tortoise love, was filmed by the BBC with a super-stellar cast of Dame Judi Dench and Dustin Hoffman playing the two neighbours who fall in love. Dahl would surely have been delighted that the best actors in the world were queuing up to appear in films of his work.

There have been a few adaptations of Roald's *The BFG* before, but the biggest to date is director Steven Spielberg's 2016 film version. This version, many years in the making and starring English actor and Oscar winner Mark Rylance in the title role of The BFG, had a budget (that's how much it cost to make) of a whooping $130 million! Wow – that's a very BIG BFG indeed.

Break a leg, Mr Dahl!

There have also been two very successful stage adaptations of Roald's brilliant books. The first was *Matilda the Musical*, which was commissioned by the Royal Shakespeare Company in 2010. It proved to be a big, big success and many productions of it have opened around the world. In fact over 50 different young actresses have played Matildas in different productions.

As well as the 2005 film, *Charlie and the Chocolate Factory* has also become a tasty treat of a stage musical. It opened in London in 2013 and was directed by Oscar winner Sam Mendes, who also directed two huge James Bond films. When tickets were released, it broke the record for the highest weekly sales ever. Talk about a golden ticket!

THE FINAL CHAPTER

Sadly, it's time to say goodbye to Mr Dahl. A few months after he finished writing *The Vicar of Nibbleswicke*, Roald was taken into hospital in Oxford. He died on 23rd November 1990 at the grand old age of 74. The funeral service was held in the church in the village of Great Missenden. Afterwards, Roald was buried on the hillside opposite Gipsy House where he spent so many years living and writing. Visitors to his grave often arrive to find a small pile of chocolate bars on his tombstone that have been left by other readers wanting to pay their respects.

But which Roald was it that had passed away? Roald the Writer? Roald the War Hero? Roald the Rude? Roald the Spy? Roald the Difficult? Roald the Dad? Roald was all these things – and more. When Roald had left school he had no idea he wanted to be a writer – but by the end of his life he was one of the most famous and successful authors on the planet! In a poll to decide the Top 100 Books of the 20th Century, Roald had four chart entries – more than any other writer.

When Roald died he left his family over three million pounds. Roald's second wife, Felicity, is in charge of looking after the books and the money. Half of the earnings from Roald's books goes to Roald Dahl's Marvellous Children's Charity – set up to help seriously ill children in the UK. The other half of the money is split between the various members of his large family. Roald's granddaughter, Sophie Dahl, started her career as a model, but soon picked up a pen to follow in Roald's famous footsteps and become a published author in her own right. And yes, the little girl in *The BFG* was named for her.

Roald's life is celebrated by the Roald Dahl Museum and Story Centre hosted in his home village, as well as a blue plaque on the site of the sweet shop where he played his horrible dead mouse trick as a kid (remember that?)

In the years since Roald's death, his books have gone on selling and selling in countries all around the world. An amazing one million copies of Roald Dahl's books are now bought each year! Different generations of children have each discovered the delights of reading Roald Dahl.

Roald's birthday on 13th September has officially become Roald Dahl Day, and each year fans around the globe celebrate his life, his characters and his books in imaginative ways.

So what is it about his children's books that make them so popular? For a start, and as we've seen, Roald worked and worked at his stories until they were as good as they could possibly be. But perhaps most importantly, Roald never forgot the people he was writing for. He didn't write his books for critics to enjoy, or for teachers, or librarians, or even parents. Roald wrote his stories for his readers. He never forgot whose side he was on during the story either – whatever the book was, Roald was always on the side of children. No wonder that to readers and fans everywhere, Roald was one of the greatest storytellers ever.